My sister Ginger has captured t
a procrastinator in this book titleu *I'd Rather Do This!"*
As children, our first part of life was mapped out for us to a
certain point, but as adults, we realize that life is not as easy
as our parents made it look; can I get a witness? There was
more happening behind the scenes that contributed to our
living a productive and balanced life. *I'd Rather Do This* will
help you discover what prevents you from being the best
you can be, and you will also discover who or what you are
allowing to push you out of alignment, how to break that
cycle and begin to live out your destiny now! If you are a
leader in any capacity, this book will bless you tremendously.
It will help you identify and avoid some of the pitfalls that
could lead to a very costly ride on the roller coaster of
procrastination, which can hinder your life, family, business
or ministry. This amazing work is a "must read!

-- Apostle Victoria Austin, Senior Pastor
Master's Touch International Ministries
Millington, Tennessee

There are many books we need in our resource libraries and
this book, *"I'd Rather Do This"*, by Prophetess Ginger Taylor
is one guide you must have. Regardless of our age we all
have had or will have bouts in this one area, procrastination,
which can be lethal to us as well as our ministries. This book
will require that you do a self-examination to identify any
area or areas where this pattern has formed or is beginning
to form, so that you can cut it off at the root before it begins
to produce fruit. If you've not seen the type of fruit Christ
promised, procrastination may be why you not receiving the
harvest that is surely there for those living as vessels of
honor.

-- Apostle Daniel Hines, Senior Pastor
City Refuge Mission Family Worship Center
Brunswick, Georgia

I'd

Rather

Do

This

———

GINGER L. JOHNSON - TAYLOR

FMG PUBLISHING
Warner Robins, Georgia

Unless otherwise indicated, Scripture is taken from The King James Version (KJV) of the Bible.

Published by FMG Publishing Company: A division of Unique Expressions
2929 Watson Blvd #118, Warner Robins, Ga 31093

Book Cover
By Davis Brenton Photography: davisbrentdphotography@gmail.com

The back of the book cover layout was done by
Unique Expressions, Warner Robins, Georgia
Email: Uniquebizness@yahoo.ocom

Printed in the United States of America
First Edition: November 2016

Library of Congress Cataloging-in-Publication Data
Taylor, Ginger L. Johnson
          I'd Rather Do This/Ginger L. Johnson-Taylor

ISBN 978-153979-642-8

1. Taylor, Ginger L. Johnson. 1965 - 2. Prophetess—United States—Encouragement.

This book is dedicated to my loving and supportive mother, my First Mentor and best friend, Mrs. Sylvia Johnson. You are the most awesome woman I know! You have always set a godly, loving, prayerful and diligent example before me. You have lived your life walking in the fullness of excellence. You did not instill in me procrastination or laziness. In fact, you taught and demonstrated to me just the opposite. You taught me what it means to work hard and to do things in a timely manner. Mom, I appreciate your example! I can't tell you how much I love and admire you. But can I say, for all the times I put things off until the last minute... it was only because I found some stuff that I'd rather do that I liked much better.

All My Love, Ginger L. Johnson – Taylor

Contents

Section I

Section II

Objective - Provide HELP and encouragement for the procrastinator as well as to those associated with the procrastinator.

Section III

Objective – to provide definitions for words used throughout the book that are necessary for the reader to know the true meaning

Acknowledgements

I'd like to first take the time to say a special thank you to my Savior and my Lord, Jesus. Who would have ever guessed that He would allow me to write on something so dangerous, so serious and expect me to have it done in "time"? Not in a million years would I have guessed that I would be entrusted with such a phenomenal task! For this I am honored and grateful. I'm even more grateful that He loves me unconditionally.

I want to thank my spiritual advisors and confidants; My sister, Pastor Victoria Austin, Sr. Pastor of The Master's Touch International; Marshall L. Graham, Bishop and Sr., Pastor of Greater New Hope Ministries COCWIH and the entire Greater New Hope Ministries Church Family; Pastors Bruce and MaShonda Moxley, Pastors of Dominion Ministries International, and the DMI Church Family; Chief Apostle Daniel T. Hines, Pastor of City of Refuge Mission Family Worship Center; Elder Henry & Judith Wilkerson; Dr. Leila Brumfield and Evangelist Joyce Temple.

I'd like to thank my editors Minister Diana Peterson and Christina Conley. You ladies ROCK! I know it's taken me forever, but I knew going into it I had a stellar team that would assist me in getting things done on a level of excellence that superseded all of my expectations. To my media team, Shanika Clowers, Felicia Green and Mr. Brenton Davis: you guys capture my visions and put them to print or publication! You are some kind of designers! Love each of you to the moon and back.

A special thank you to a group of ladies who constantly pray for me and sow seed into the wildest visions that I have to advance the Kingdom of God - Sharon Proctor, Minister Linda Clark, Dr. Denise Noel, Nedra Webster, Greta Graham, Marjorie Harris, Laura Lee Phillippi and MIT Shaneika Williams. Thank you ladies for constantly sowing into my ministry and dreams.

To that group of sisters, known as the Fab Five (that includes me), Prissy McDaniel–Ellis, Lisa Poller–Horton, Sharon Wesley–Fluker and Toni Taylor–Russell: Well sisters, I think you can all verify that I'm a certified professional at what I do, especially in the area of *Procrastination*. Thank you for loving me, believing in me and supporting me for over forty years. There isn't a bond or love that can be any closer.

I would also like to thank a very special group of people who have absolutely no idea that they were all a part of a special Kingdom project. I know they didn't sign up to be, but ultimately they had no choice. This group of special ladies worked for an agency called Community Care Services Program; namely Doris Carter, Darienne Schuller, Ingrid Marshall, Rosa Baldwin, Adrienne Holloway, Shaneji Ward, Chantelle Sams, Dorothy Wilson, Viva Elbert, Dr. Lucianna Green, Liz Hutchings, Wanda Green, Kim Davis, Marjorie Harris, Shirley Nix, Lavella Head, Beneikia Johnson and Taesha Ward. There were a ton of days that I know I drove them absolutely crazy! There were a few more that were on board, but this group right here - I had a firsthand opportunity to drive them *nuts!* I love each and every one of them and I always feel the love in return, when they talked about me, told me off, helped me out and worked my nerves. I'm serious! It was a love, hate relationship like none I've ever fostered and it was centered on my ability to put things off to the absolute very last minute.

Then there are those that love me unconditionally, but totally understand my issue: my phenomenal mother, Sylvia Johnson; brother & sister-in law William & Lorraine Johnson; my children, Gitoya & Jonathan Lane and Kinan Taylor, my adorable grand-princesses Braelyn, Jael, Skylar and Kai and my goddaughters, Keila Graham and Sierra Alford.

And last but certainly not least, I want to thank my rock and my go-to guy for everything that ails me – my husband – Isaac Taylor, Jr. Honey, I know I'm a work in progress. I realize there are times you have really plea bargained with the Lord, but He begged you to stick it out with me. I just want to say thank you from my heart for never giving up on me, even when you may have been justified in doing so. Your tolerance of my procrastination to my pack rat maintenance has to be a supernatural gift from God! I love you to smithereens and appreciate you more than words can express. I just want to say - the best is yet to come!

Forward

The short conversation by text went something like this, "I'll have the forward (to your book) to you by tomorrow," and she replied, "Yay." I'm sorry to say I didn't have the forward to her by the deadline that I *gave*, and I'm ashamed to admit this was a conversation that I had with the author of this book, regarding writing the forward for this book. Wow! How desperately I need this book, and if you're honest with yourself, there is a good chance that you need this book as well.

I'd Rather Do This, is not only a book but a "shovel" in print that will cause you to dig deep introspectively in order to reveal to yourself "The Why" that has been preventing you from moving on in life to *your next* - Your next accomplishment, your next promotion, your next... As I began to read the first several chapters, suddenly a personal revelation hit me, "How many people who love me and whom I love have I hurt, let down, stolen from in some way because of my procrastination?" "How have I stunted my own growth through my procrastination?" I sincerely thought that waiting was not hurting me or anyone else; boy was I wrong!

Ginger Taylor does a masterful job of exposing the poison of procrastination that is slowly killing the future dreams of many. You are worth this book. If procrastination is a problem for you, then this is the book for you. No more excuses. The world is waiting for the better you to manifest and the manifestation begins *right now*. Yes, right now!

Pastor Bruce Moxley Jr.
Dominion Ministries International (DMI)
Dayton, Ohio

Introduction

This delightful book is going to get all the way under your skin. It's purposefully designed to do just that! The writing of this book has been put off for so long because well....that's what the book is about - putting things off. Procrastination!!! There! I said it - that bad word that no one ever wants to do anything about. If you are reading this book, you're doing so for one of a few top five reasons – here're the first three:

1 - You love me and just want to show support;

2 - You may already be inducted into to the "The Procrastinator's Guild;" or

3 - You are tired of making excuses and you're ready to implement the necessary changes in your life to get things done!

About eight years ago, I was blessed with what I would label or call at that time, my dream job; at least in my mind that's what I had conjured it up to be. By profession I'm a nurse, an LPN to be exact and a pretty good one at that. However, I have a few personal issues with the entire nursing thing. No. 1 - I don't particularly enjoy having to wear uniforms every day. No. 2 - Have you seen the nursing shoes lately? They look like boats or fat clogs and I don't care for those either. Can someone say fashion diva? At any rate, the job was created just for me!

On this particular job, I was able to wear everyday fashionable business attire! And if you enjoy fashion as

15

much as I do, then automatically this places this job in the "dream job" category. My other joy, as it pertains to the job, was the fact that the job required me to interact with the elderly population. I'm pretty good working with the older crew. I honestly believe I have a gift of love and compassion for the elderly. Caring for them, spending time with them and gleaning wisdom from their lives, has always been a tremendous delight to me. But the story takes a huge left turn at the fork in the road because the job not only required me doing assessments on the individuals but it eventually thrust me over into the social work category.

The assessments were to determine needs that the individual may have and whether or not the needs were being met. I was also responsible for determining if the individual remained eligible to stay on the program to receive services that were arranged by our staff. Needless to say, all of the above required me to document things, get papers signed, complete reports and send them to the necessary companies that would help provide the support that the elderly individuals and their families needed.

Well, what started out as a dream job quickly became a nightmare filled with a barrage of paper work!!! What was worse was I only had a limited amount of time to get all of the work completed. To this day, I have no idea how I lasted as long as I did because the work became so tedious, stressful, overwhelming and frequently mundane. It was constant chaos. It was more than that; it was a viscous cycle that seemed to be never ending. There was no one way to do the job; people did whatever worked for them as long as the work got done within the time constraints given. The problem for me was since there was no one way to do the job, I tried incorporating a little of everyone's best ideas to assist me in having a better flow and completing everything in a timely manner. However, I could never find a way to get caught up or stay ahead. It was a hot mess! I felt as if I was suffocating or drowning nearly every day.

Over the course of time, I had to go in and see the program manager. On one particular day we were discussing my evaluation. Now let me just admit, I knew I was doing a substandard job. If you let me tell it from my perspective, it just wasn't my fault. I felt that the training and overall program lacked structure and organization. There was no real – true order regarding the job. Everyone just did their own thing, and at the end of the day, no two people operated using the same system. So, during my evaluation, a few of my marks were kind of low. I have a signature statement that I learned from a little red headed director of nursing a long time ago, and it simply states, "What in the Thunda!" I'm kinda known for saying it now. It's really appropriate for crap like getting bad marks on your performance evaluation that you don't agree with. My boss proceeded to tell me that my organizational skills could really stand to come up a notch. Well, duh! Ya think? Everyone around me was doing this job a million different ways. A little bit of all of their ways seemed to be working well for them at the time. They just never worked that well for me.

I wasn't accustomed to getting low performance appraisals. I figured if I wanted to keep the job, perhaps I'd better come up with something that would assist me in being more organized so that I could get things done in a timely manner. Prior to meeting the deadlines, audits had to be done on all of the files submitted and corrections had to be made if any errors were discovered. When I first started working with the company, I was given sixty days to complete seeing the individual, submitting all of the work, getting documents to the physician and getting them back, audits completed, corrections made, forms completed submitted and submitted to multiple entities providing support and for billing purposes, etc. With all of that, there were yet deadlines that had to be met. *Man!* I was trying so hard. But the harder I tried it seemed the further I would get behind. *At the rate I was going, I always placed everyone at the point of a cardiac arrest.*

The first year or so, I guess it's pretty safe to say that my program manager must have just felt sorry for me or had mercy on me. Maybe it was just the favor of God. All I know is I was hanging on by sheer threads. I received my share of low performance evaluations, and finally after one of those things, I decided rather than assess the system and others, *I would take a strong hard look at me.* I began to look at the pattern of my work ethic over the years as it pertained to turning in reports. I traced my patterns and habits all the way back to middle school when I would wait until the night before to complete a written project. I can safely say that I continued those practices all the way through college. The thought alone was pretty sad that I could not think of one time that I had ever submitted a paper early. In fact, I had never utilized my time wisely to complete projects with deadlines. *I would always calculate getting the job done down to the very last minute.* This thought and practice is what I would say got me inducted into "The Procrastinator's Guild."

Once I made that discovery, I began to look at my life as a whole to see how I conducted other matters of business such as bill paying, house cleaning, appointments, engagements and the like. In every situation, and in most circumstances, I was either late or waited until the last possible moment to act or respond. I was really in awe of my pattern of behavior. Up until that point, it really seemed harmless *until it became embarrassing*. I had gotten away with doing things at the last moment and had actually done jobs or written papers well. However, that wasn't happening at this job. My last minute escapades were creating increased stress for other people and jeopardizing the potential care for the clients I had been entrusted to assist. I was creating undue stress for myself and it was truly beginning to affect my health. My blood pressure was sky high; I barely got any good sleep or rest for that matter. I looked tired all the time and stayed sluggish.

What I would say or do to justify my actions was nothing more than an excuse. *Excuses* are "tools of incompetence, used to build monuments of nothingness, and those who specialize in them seldom accomplish anything," according to the Urban Dictionary. The dictionary definds excuses "to serve as an apology or justification for; justify." The Bible equates a procrastinator with a slothful person, a slacker, a loafer. When excuses are given in lieu of doing something that you truly had ample time to finish or complete, it sounds outlandish, preposterous, and ridiculous beyond reason, and quite honestly, makes no sense to the person to whom you're providing the excuse.

Just read this to yourself and ponder it for a moment. *The slothful man saith, there is a lion in the way; a lion is in the streets.* (Prov. 26: 13 KJV). *"Loafers say, 'It's dangerous out there! Tigers are prowling the streets!' and then pull the covers back over their heads."* (Prov. 26: 13 MSG). *"The slothful man saith, 'There is a lion without, I shall be slain in the streets."* (Prov. 22: 13 KJV). *"The loafer says, 'There's a lion on the loose! If I go out I'll be eaten alive!'"* (Prov. 22: 13 MSG). The entire statement sounds just as farfetched. That's really how excuses sound in the ears of those to whom we give them when they know that, in terms of time, you've really been allotted an ample amount of time to get the job or project done – had you taken care of it like you were supposed to.

After I identified the issue that I had, I was impressed to find out if I was actually the only one on the job who struggled with completing tasks in a timely fashion. Was I the ONLY ONE who procrastinated; or were there others? To my surprise, there were several others. I found within the office that I had some kindred spirits. The sad part was no one really had a remedy to fix the problem. So I began to study the issue from a biblical and practical standpoint in hopes that it would help somebody.

Many of us in the procrastination family will put off things until the very last second of the day, but by the time you finish reading this book you may be persuaded to try something a little different. In fact, you may rather want to do this; versus that. See you at the end of the journey.

CHAPTER ONE

What is Procrastination?

Let's get down to business. There is so much to say about this subject that it's hard to decide where to begin. What I will not do is assume that you know certain things. Therefore, I'm going to take the time to develop a glossary for you along the way. One of the first things that I want to establish is that "procrastination" has some kin folks, if you will, that play a big part in a grander scheme of things. Those kin folks are sleep and laziness. All procrastinators aren't lazy; in fact, most procrastinators are busy little bees. They are generally just busy doing the things they

Objective
Provide a clear, concise description of a procrastinator and the mindset of one who procrastinates.

would *rather do* versus the needful thing that they *should do*.

So, what exactly is procrastination? Procrastination – putting off or delaying, especially something requiring immediate attention (Dictionary). Avoiding doing something for as long as possible, sometimes not doing it at all (UD).

Here are some other definitions those individuals who struggle with or in this area rattled off to me:

- Voluntarily delaying an intended course of action despite expecting to be worse off for the delay.

-Waiting until the last minute to do something.

-Putting something off.

-Not doing something - even though you know it's the wrong choice not to do it, you still choose not to.

One of the objectives in writing this book is to get a better understanding of why we consistently put things off and the ramifications of doing so. You see, for the most part, we put things off in our activities of daily living; things such as work, bills, chores, errands, maintenance, school work, applications, etc. It's generally summed up in our minds that putting things off until later won't hurt anyone because the intention is to eventually get it done. I mean seriously, why waste all this "good ole time" doing something you really don't feel like doing or don't even like to do? Let's be honest, during that time that you are putting off a task you are probably doing something else that is much rather preferred.

There is another list of things that we have a tendency to put off, other things that are extremely crucial and critical such as exercising, conversations that need to be had, going to the doctor, changing our environment or circle of acquaintances, following our dreams, exploring our gifts and talents, taking that big risk to do something at which we are really great or perhaps doing the will of the Father! *Need I go on*? In these instances we use a different set of excuses and we continue to entertain the thought, "it probably wouldn't make a difference if I did it or not anyway."

Here is one of the realest things you are ever going to hear as it pertains to procrastination: *you know when you are doing it!* There is no doubt in my mind that you are NOT ignorant to when you are procrastinating. You may not want to call it that word at the exact moment you're engaging in procrastination, because it makes you feel a little guilty or "some type of way." Ultimately, you are very much aware of the business, chore, homework, assignment, Kingdom Assignment etc. that you are supposed to be completing; but for whatever reason - you've opted not to do it.

Simply put, when you put things off until another day or time, or simply delay taking action on something that you are "aware" that you need to do, means you fit the most classic and text book definition of a procrastinator.

- So let's stop for a moment and do a self assessment. In a journal or on a slip of paper, list some things that you know you wait until the last minute to do.

- What do you do instead or in place of what you should be doing?

- Have you ever asked yourself why you are putting things off?

- What kind of rationale do you come up with once you've tried to reason why you aren't doing the needful thing?

- What is usually the outcome of waiting until the last minute or putting something off that you need to be doing?

- The thing or things that you are putting off, are they affecting anyone else other than you?

- If they are, what is your attitude or disposition about the effect your action is having on others?

- Have you considered the overall damage that putting things off is doing "to you?"

- What would happen if you took a different approach and actually did the task in a timely manner?

- What do you think it would feel like?

- Are you willing to give it a try - doing a task on time or even early for that matter?

- Are you ready for a change?

When I think of how procrastinating has affected me over the years, it really is a hard pill to swallow. I'm of the opinion that when you are younger the rationale that you feed yourself to get it done later really makes a whole lot of sense. However, as you age and you never do anything to rectify the behavior, those excuses of putting things off really don't make a whole lot of sense any more. It goes back to the category of excuses.

The word "Procrastination" is not found in the King James Version of the Bible. Yet, words that are synonymous with procrastination are found in the word of God – words such as:

Slothful   Slow   Sluggard   Idle

These words are found in scripture and in many instances imply putting things off or not completing them at all. Look at this glossary of words that are synonymous with procrastination:

Block	Put on the back burner
Delay	Put on hold
Detain	Put on ice
Extend	Set aside
Give rain check	Shelve
Hold up	Stall

Impede	Slow
Lay over	Suspend
Lengthen	Table
Postpone	Wave

definitions can be found in the back of the book

     I want us to take some time to examine some of these words throughout the book and take a hard look at why we put things off. In examining why we put things off, it may help us in making a decision to do things differently and encourage us to make the necessary changes to be productive. The truth is *procrastination is not your friend!* I believe everyone has put something off at some point in life. You've taken your time, delayed doing something, or put it on the back burner because it wasn't on your list of top priorities. You've postponed something! For whatever reason, you managed to shelve it or set it aside.

     Well my friend, those are just fancy, smancy words to say "you procrastinated." Here's a truth of which you should grab hold that is extremely relevant; there is a shift that takes place when procrastination has become a way of life. When you use a last minute approach as a means to function rather than own the area of negligence, you have given place to a habit. Habits that are not dealt with become nothing more than a stronghold – a way of thinking that requires deliverance and immediate change. Now we are talking about something spiritual that really is

designed overall to keep you from getting to your next--
your purpose.

> *"Anyone can do any amount of work*
> *providing it isn't the work he is supposed to*
> *be doing at that moment."*

Robert Bunchley

Stop procrastinating – starting tomorrow! Not! Don't wait another day! Begin to pray for change in your life NOW! "Boast not thyself of tomorrow; for thou knowest not what a day may bring forth." Proverbs 27:1 (KJV). "Don't boast about tomorrow, for you don't know what a day might bring." Proverbs 27:1 (NIV).

Scripture encourages us not to brag or boast on the next day as to what's going to happen. Clearly we don't have that information as to what will or won't happen. That is part of the habit of a procrastinator; we mentally boast, plan, or calculate what can be accomplished the next day. We entertain conversations with ourselves as to what all we can accomplish at a later time that usually involves the next day. The Word of God has relieved us of duty in that area, because we don't know what a day might bring. We don't know the ins and outs of the day. Yet, we function as if we do by waiting until the last minute or just stalling or taking a rain check on a project, and thus life.

I interviewed with countless people about the topic of procrastination to gain insight on various mindsets and patterns of thought concerning the matter. I met with those who were confessed procrastinators and those who were just the opposite – 'do it now' people. What was interesting was the fact that because I can identify as a procrastinator, I can truly admit that I understood the rationale and psyche of all fellow procrastinators.

Allow me to let you enter the mind of the procrastinator. In the mind of the procrastinator, the task at hand often seems mundane, uneventful, time consuming, extra (to say the least), not that big of a deal, and in most cases – though relevant, in the mind of a procrastinator it's not a major priority on the list of things to do. There is always something else that we would rather do.

Now, this doesn't mean that it isn't a major priority to *someone*, but at any given time, it's just not a priority to us – the procrastinators. When it boils down to livelihood, procrastinators may very well understand the importance of the job and the function of that job. Please don't get it twisted, a procrastinator is more often than not very intelligent, a multi-tasker of events, projects, situations and circumstances. However, selfishness and lack of immediate urgency, diminishes the priority of the task that needs to be done and places it behind the "things" that the procrastinator chooses as more importance. I can hear you screaming at me now... how dare you be on someone's payroll and place their task behind your own! Well I can tell you from research and experience that it goes along with the identification of a procrastinator.

I worked for a company for seven and a half years. While doing so, I continued to do ministry work full time. I traveled, I preached, I facilitated, I strategized, I wrote curricula, I assisted fellow clergy in completing tasks, I sang, I prayed, I wrote, I created programs, I hosted conferences, I visited the sick and shut in.....and continue to do those things to date. However, the difference between now and then is that back then I had a job that had deadlines. They were referred to as "standards of promptness." According to policy and procedure, things had to be completed within a certain amount of time – 24 hours, three days, 30 days, 60 days, etc. Needless to say, I fell short on countless occasions. What was crazy was, in order not to feel guilty, every time I traveled out of town, state or country, I would take the work with me. I didn't get a thing done, but I took it with every intention of trying to tackle some work in between doing the thing that I love more than anything, which is ministry.

Was I wrong? Of course I was! But you would be absolutely shocked at the people who continue to do, if not the same thing, similar things. They do the thing that they enjoy – what they'd rather do - over and above the thing that is required. I even had some people tell me that they would do things they didn't even like to avoid doing the thing that they knew needed to be done. An example would be a project for work or an assignment for school that is needed and required; well, the procrastinator would clean up or perform mindless tasks just to avoid doing the project or writing the paper. The sad part is, in instances like this the rationale is a typical, direct response like, 'I just don't feel like it' or 'I'll do it later' or 'I'll get around to it.' Then you will get other responses that are just flat out lies and excuses as a cover up.

With my previous job, when I traveled somehow I would factor in the time that I could fit in doing my work and have it done by the time it was due to be turned in. When I tell you that every single time I took work with me, I got very little accomplished and still would end up waiting until the very last minute to even begin trying to get the work done. In the mind of a procrastinator, there is this thing we do with time that still has me baffled. It's as if we have a special formula to calculate how much time it should take to finish a project. It looks something like this....

Example of Procrastinator's Math:

"One report should take 43 minutes; I have 20 reports – so 20 x 43 = 860 minutes divided by 60 = 15 hours of total work. So if I break that down by three days I need 5 hours a day to have it done on time. I'll do 2.5 hours in the morning and 2.5 hours in the evening and I should have it completed by Wednesday to turn in by the deadline."

Now the only problem with this is the *deadline*! It's just that - The *deadline*! There is no in between, no consideration for mistakes, no consideration taken for any problems that can go wrong, no consideration of others in the event something needs to be audited. Now every single procrastinator doesn't go by this fictitious mathematical equation, but every procrastinator has a personalized mathematical equation of time that they use in order to determine down to the exact minute how long it will take to accomplish the task that they have in front of them by the time it is due. Isn't that crazy? Doesn't it drive you crazy - if you are not a procrastinator - to know this type of inside information about *us*? We honestly haven't been able to help it - up until now.

Well, don't be so hard on yourself or - if you're not a procrastinator – don't give up on us yet, at least not now anyway. Let's make it to the end of the journey and see if you aren't persuaded and encouraged to make a change or assist us in changing.

Note(s) to self from this chapter

_____
_____
_____
_____
_____
_____
_____
_____
_____
_____
_____
_____
_____

Write your own personal daily affirmations

_____
_____
_____
_____
_____
_____
_____
_____
_____
_____
_____
_____
_____

CHAPTER TWO

The *Pile* Up

Because I have struggled with procrastination for so long, it's quite easy to detect that issue in others. It reminds me of any other disease. Procrastination comes with its own set of signs and symptoms. I can laugh at it now, because I've chosen to confront this area of weakness in my life. As I've stated earlier, no one knows better than *you* when you are procrastinating! I want to make you keenly aware that although you know you are putting something off, the signs and symptoms of the disease of procrastination alert everyone else that you are putting something off.

Objective

Provide readers with some insights and the answers to why a procrastinator won't change - who and what hinders that process.

What are the signs and symptoms of procrastination? (Hold on to your hat for this one!)

The signs and symptoms are:

1. EXCUSES

2. EXCUSES

3. EXCUSES

Those are the top three signs and symptoms. Now the byproducts of the signs and symptoms are unfinished work and projects, disorder in many areas of your life, stress, tension, anxiety, unrest with decisions, constant thinking and strategizing as to how to get out of this hole you have dug for yourself.

The sad part is thinking about it never gets the job done. It's really just another form of procrastination that makes you feel as if you're making progress... because you're thinking. *Sike!* That, my friend, is another trick of the enemy of your soul. A thought with no action is just that, *a thought*.

A Moment or Two of Transparency

In Chapter One, I asked you to list some things that you wait until the last minute to do. Okay, here is one of the things I loathe doing – laundry! Now, while I love pretty, clean clothes, I cannot stand washing, drying, folding and putting away my clothes. Some may constitute that as being lazy, but I'm far from that! I just don't like doing laundry. There is always something else that I'd rather be doing.

Here's my excuse: *it takes too long!* That's an entire day of that! *Ugh!* First you've got to sort the clothes, then you've got to load the washer, wait for them to wash, then load them in the dryer, once they are dry you've got to fold them all up and put them in their proper places. *I hate it!* That may not be anywhere near an issue that you have. However, have you ever gone to someone's home or in the bedroom of your child and there are clothes piled up to the ceiling because they won't fold and put them away? They aren't necessarily nasty or lazy; they just don't like doing the whole laundry thing! Well ultimately, if I never do the laundry, it just piles up.... The dirty clothes pile up if I don't wash them and the clean clothes pile up if I don't fold and put them away.

Subsequently, when I begin to look around the room I begin to calculate the length of time it's going to take me to get all of it done, because now I've let it *pile up and it begins to feel overwhelming!* The idea of completing the task begins to make me feel and experience anxiety. Now let's factor in someone coming over to visit or a big event that perhaps I may want to host at my home.... Now I've got twice the amount of work to do and triple the amount of stress and anxiety when I could have just done a little bit at a time to begin with and not have to deal with this gigantic elephant of a chore!

Well, I used the scenario of *laundry*, but in all actuality this is the vicious cycle that many of us find ourselves in when it comes down to procrastinating. The scenario may vary but the cause and effect is the same. We experience the frustration of a task that we don't particularly enjoy, put it off and put it off and nothing gets done until we are forced to do it. We make all the excuses in the world, but the task at hand still is not dealt with. Then it piles up and we make more and more excuses to not deal with it, almost to the point of embarrassment. By the time we choose to deal with it, we are in way over our heads and it's like, 'let's just take a match and burn it all!'

Here's another area that we may or may not have in common – Mail! I just need to know, do you receive junk mail? That is the most aggravating thing in the world to me!! You would think that I would just throw it away when it comes in the house, but instead, it goes into a basket and the mail continues to accumulate until the basket is full. Now I've got the pile up!! Who wants to sit and sort for junk mail? Ugh! That is so annoying and, trust me, I can think of a ton of things that I'd rather do than to sort through junk mail. So you know the routine, it builds and builds…. Now I'm loathing having to go through it more than ever. It's not like I don't have the time to do it; I just don't want to. I'd rather do something else.

This may seem a tad unrealistic to some, but it is the life of a procrastinator! Ask me how I know. Every one of your emotions is real. Now imagine if you're talking about something other than laundry, something like a term paper, a project, bills, or anything that involves you completing a task, and there may be deadlines involved. That is a tale with a different spin! It's one thing to put off doing something that doesn't affect anyone but you, but it's another thing when there is something at stake like your livelihood, your credit score, your GPA or perhaps your graduation or possible promotion. Don't get it twisted, you've got some pretty successful procrastinators in some very high places in this life, but it doesn't mean that the struggle is any different. Some have just mastered the art of dealing with the *"Pile Up."* However, I would venture to say that even those that may be in higher up places aren't as high as they could be, because procrastination ultimately costs you. It can cost you opportunities at times and promotions at other times. Truth be known, those recognized excuses have consequences and repercussions that can hinder you immensely.

Check out these scriptures from the book of Proverbs.

> *"I went past the field of a sluggard, past the vineyard of someone who has no sense; thorns had come up everywhere, the ground was covered with weeds, and the stone wall was in ruins."* *Prov. 24: 30 – 31 (NIV)*

> Another version says '*I walked by the field of a lazy person, the vineyard of one lacking sense. I saw that it was overgrown with thorns. It was covered with weeds, and its walls were broken down. Then, as I looked and thought about it, I learned this lesson; A little extra sleep, a little more slumber, a little folding of the hands to rest - and*

poverty will pounce on you like a bandit;
scarcity will attack you like an armed
robber. "Prov. 24: 30 – 33 (NLT)

"The Slacker does not plow during planting
season; at harvest time he looks, and there
is nothing." Prov. 20: 4 (HSB)

There is so much to be said concerning all of these marvelous scriptures. The insights are unreal! One of the first things that I want to share with you is that there is a difference between procrastination and laziness.

First of all what is a slacker / sluggard?

Slacker - a person who evades his or her duty or work; shirker.

Sluggard - a person who is habitually inactive or lazy.

Holy Spirit revealed it to me this way: "Lazy can; but won't. Procrastination does; but later, eventually."

"Laziness induces deep sleep, and a lazy
person will go hungry." Prov. 19: 15 (HSB)

"A lazy person sleeps soundly – and goes
hungry." Prov. 19: 15 (NLT)

"Some people are so lazy that they won't even lift a finger to feed themselves." Prov. 19: 24 (NLT)

Most procrastinators are really busy, diligent people but, in the minds of others, have misplaced priorities. To the true procrastinator, the thing that they have chosen to do, believe it or not, *is a priority to the procrastinator.* It is the thing that they would rather be doing as well as the thing that is of the utmost importance to them at that time.

The problem with that is that when things are not accomplished in a timely manner and there is a point of accountability, the procrastinator can be mistaken for one who is lazy. That is almost as bad as being misdiagnosed by a physician. Some of the symptoms may manifest the same, but there is a major difference between someone who puts off something until later and one who won't lift a finger to complete a task. However, the Pileup can be so overwhelming that the procrastinator may feel like giving up or giving in, but they are driven to get it done, even at the last minute, at the risk of losing sleep, social activities and the likes.

Putting things off that really need to be done is an absolute mindset. Watch this! When you are in need of a job and you choose to look for one "later", that's a mind-set. When you have health issues and need to lose weight, but rehearse in your mind... I'll start "tomorrow"... that's a mind-set. When you're of a certain age and know that there are test that you should take for preventive measures, but verbalize "I'll do it later".... That's a mindset.

Putting things of importance off is truly a *stronghold*. That *stronghold* can cost you so much. It can cost you your life in the natural as well as in the spirit. There are people that I know, that had they gone to get a check-up, they would probably be alive and well today. There are those whose marriages would be in tact had they taken the time to find employment rather than chill at the house and play video games because they preferred to look for a job later. And the list goes on!

I've come to learn that people do what they want to do. If you don't make certain things a priority, then they won't be. Until you choose to take an honest look at what really matters, then you will keep putting things on the back burner. That is not a healthy practice; although, the enemy of our soul wants us to feel that we are out-smarting "the system." Do you know how many people have believed that they could outsmart "the system" – a system of authority, parents, husbands, wives, teachers, bosses, IRS, bill collectors...oh and let's not forget the most powerful of them all - GOD?

We have heard the old adage "how do you eat an elephant?" The answer is "one bite at a time." But for the procrastinator, we try to eat the entire elephant all at one time, especially because we have let it pile up. Breaking down a huge task or assignment into small, manageable pieces is a safe, practical, reasonable, methodical way of doing things properly. It affords us the opportunity to have checks and balances in place. It gives us the time span needed to make corrections and perfect the project or assignment. Operating in this orderly fashion ensures that we are not stressed, anxious and full of regret that the proper attention was not given, but it was managed properly and the product is a true representation of the excellence that we want to portray.

> *"Take a lesson from the ants, you lazy-bones. Learn from their ways and be wise! Even though they have no prince, governor, or ruler to make them work, they labor hard all summer, gathering food for the winter. But you, lazybones, how long will you sleep, a little more slumber, a little folding of the hands to rest – poverty will pounce on you like a bandit; scarcity will attack you like an armed robber." Prov. 6:6-11 (NLT)*

Note(s) to self from this chapter

_____
_____
_____
_____
_____
_____
_____
_____
_____
_____
_____
_____

Write your own personal daily affirmations

_____
_____
_____
_____
_____
_____
_____
_____
_____
_____
_____
_____

CHAPTER THREE

Enabling *Behaviors* and Habits

Seeds are small things that grow and develop into larger things or into a multiplicity of things, such as thoughts, ideas or habits. When we start out early in life with someone making things very easy for us, so much so that we bypass learning life lessons of preparation and disciplines, we can easily gravitate toward embracing a habit as handicapping and paralyzing as procrastination.

Objective

Provide readers with some insights and the answers to why a procrastinator won't change -who and what hinders that process.

I shared with you the fact that I was active in school with many extra-curricular activities. Once I began participating with certain activities after school, I would get home later in the evenings at times. Oftentimes things that may have been in order for me to do – my responsibilities, my mother eventually did them for me. That doesn't seem too uncommon now does it? Well, it should be. 'Why?' you may ask. First of all, this becomes a slick way for procrastinator to get over on others and to develop negative habits. You see, procrastinators operate with a certain level of assumption. In other words, the typical procrastinator thinks, 'if I take my time doing something that I really don't want to do anyway, I know that eventually it's going to get done by someone else; it just won't get done by me.' To some that may seem a little funny. Ultimately, the person picking up the slack in order to be helpful or supportive is *enabling* the procrastinator to a very large degree.

Enable is defined as,

: to make (someone or something) able *to do* or *to be* something

: to make (something) possible, practical, or easy

: to cause (a feature or capability of a computer) to be active or available for use

When Does Procrastination Creep In

Speaking of seeds, when and where does procrastination begin? How old were you when you began establishing the habit of putting things off until later? As I look back over my life, I think about the things that I used to love doing. I always enjoyed sports and most outdoor activities. I was a life guard. I played tennis. I played softball. I loved the game of basketball. I played basketball from junior high school all the way through college. I even played for the Castle Air Force Base Basketball Team.

So as a youngster playing ball, I would come home and practically all of my chores were done before I left home. I had to make my bed, clean my room, and make sure that the bathroom was cleaned behind me. My mother and father did not play that dirty house mess! Growing up in my parents' home, Saturday was the day for getting down and dirty with the household chores. *As long as I had that accountability, there was no problem*. When I went off to college, it was the same way. I had roommates who were neat freaks, therefore, I kept up with my home training and my dorm room stayed neat and clean. As long as I was held strictly accountable, procrastination had little to no place.

Unhealthy Routine Changes: Can Start Procrastination

Now let's back up a little. I asked when and where did procrastination begin – right? Well for me, it began with writing those "papers!" You know the ones I'm talking about... initially it was the little book report. I'd have to read the book, and then ultimately do a report on the book that I had read. I was given a certain amount of time to read the book and a deadline to turn in the paper. If the book was interesting, I'd knock out the reading but I would still postpone doing the report part. If the book was boring, I'd buy the Cliffs Notes, filibuster through a paper and kind of wing it. I would still make great grades. That, my friend, was the beginning of practicing the art of procrastination.

In my mind it just did not seem as though writing a paper should take that long. So, I figured, why waste all this good time doing homework when I could be doing something so much more enjoyable. I spent the good majority of my time talking on the phone to my boyfriend. It's sad to say, but that's what would occupy my precious and unredeemable time! My little relationship was a top priority. I was that way in high school, college, the military and not a whole lot has changed. I'm that way now on some days.

I can admit this stuff now because God is helping me to walk through my deliverance process and I, in turn, want to HELP YOU! I never purposed in my heart to be a procrastinator. In fact, I didn't readily admit to being a procrastinator until I purchased the lie of the enemy! And what lie am I referring to? The one that says "you're smart; you can outwit them! It won't take all day, you can do it LATER." Now mind you, the proof was in the pudding. I was smart. I had a lovely GPA. I did complete most projects at the last minute and did well on them. But the lie I was buying was bigger than just a term paper and a grade. It was a mind-set, one that could, I believe, hinder me from attaining all that God truly intended for me to accomplish.

Responsibility Reduces Procrastination

As parents, if we make things completely easy for our children without ever making them follow through with their responsibilities, we are in danger of raising procrastinating adults, and in many cases, *lazy* adults. They become dependent upon others to eventually pick up the slack; or perhaps, they embrace a mindset that everything is going to be handed to them on a silver platter. However, that is not a realistic picture of life. There is nothing worse than seeing a grown person dependent on their parents for every little thing because when they were children the parents did the thing that was seemingly hard or unpleasant for the child instead of demanding that the child complete the task with excellence – in a timely manner. The parent also makes excuses for the child, thus the beginning of a learned behavior – a habit.

This is not how every person that is a procrastinator gets their beginning. However, if you trace your history back to the beginning of when you started practicing the art of procrastination, I would venture to say that something or someone set you on the path of *"putting stuff off"* and you rationalized why that was a marvelous idea and you should have thought of it sooner.

As I look back over my life, I'm amazed at the different procrastinators I've met. It's funny because we are open to suggestions, but for the most part, we don't take to criticism regarding our "issue" too well. It's horrible. I can't explain why we are that way other than to say it's like any other "addiction" – you first have to admit that you have a problem. Most procrastinators are aware that they are procrastinators, yet herein rests the problem: unless our habit has caused us some grief, there really isn't any reason to change the way we've always done things. We don't want to change "right now" – we will do it later. You see, the lie we believe is "I work better under pressure." We truly believe that we do our finest work at the last minute.

We usually come out on top looking stellar! Until it reaches the point that we are convicted or embarrassed by our own errors or ways, we won't initiate methods or habits to develop new disciplines.

Examining my own life, I began to think of all the people that would enable my behavior and that of other fellow procrastinators. One of the ways that parents, bosses, teachers, managers, spouses, and creditors enable procrastinators is by extending to us *"grace,"* yes grace. Yes, that's right... *grace,* approval, favor, mercy, pardon, special favor, privilege. Those that enable procrastinators do themselves a tremendous disservice. I understand the need to extend grace, but what happens is oftentimes procrastinators only put off the task to extend up and through the grace period. Professional procrastinators are masterful at using a grace period to put off a task even further.

After speaking with over thirty people about their thoughts on procrastination, most, if not all, agreed that they have a tendency to still wait until the last minute to perform a task, in spite of the extended grace period given. The mindset of a procrastinator is to take advantage of grace periods by further delaying production instead of taking the opportunity to complete the task well under the newly extended timeline with a greater degree of excellence. Although grace is extended as means to provide help, the procrastinator has a tendency to prolong the task even further, thus being enabled to procrastinate even more.

Note(s) to self from this chapter

_____
_____
_____
_____
_____
_____
_____
_____
_____
_____
_____
_____
_____

Write your own personal daily affirmations

_____
_____
_____
_____
_____
_____
_____
_____
_____
_____
_____
_____
_____

CHAPTER FOUR

Rush *Hour*

Objective

Describe the measure, the length, and the adrenaline that is experienced when trying to get the project done. Playfully sharing the things that procrastinators don't anticipate when they wait until the last minute to fulfill obligations.

It's amazing the things that we as procrastinators do when we have waited until *the last minute*. Think about a few of these instances – late for work, appointments, church, deadlines, dates, interviews, invitations, parties, court, etc.

Now if we take these and begin to break them down we will find that there are a lot of similar emotions that we experience with each of these areas. Let's take a peek, shall we?

For all of the aforementioned, if we are late and we have to drive to get there, we normally find ourselves speeding. Now when this happens, we position ourselves for tickets (which cost money), accidents (which can cost lives), forgetting (which can yield embarrassment), and loss of opportunities (which can cost promotions or money). There are always consequences and repercussions for our last-minute dashes. We don't like to admit it, but it's true. Do you know how embarrassing it is to waltz into a room of people expecting to interview you and you have the wrong resume? Or perhaps, in your haste to get dressed, you put on mismatched shoes or earrings? Then there's the case of other documents that you may need to present, but you don't have them because you were rushing and did not adequately prepare, so you forgot them.

Think of the opportunities that were missed – deadlines to turn in scholarship applications (how do you pay for college now?), deadlines to apply for a position (now you don't have a job), deadlines to return merchandise to get a refund or exchange (so now you're stuck with a bunch of crap you don't even need or want.)

Here's the tip on deadlines. Deadlines are nothing more than windows of opportunities. Have you ever noticed how jobs are posted in the newspaper, online, in the office, at the school or wherever? Those postings are only there for a short period of time; they have an opening and a closing date. When we are not focused and prepared, and when we procrastinate and do things that are just irrelevant time wasters, we have a tendency to miss those opportunities. What's sad is there was really no need to miss them. Priorities should been established and followed. It's all in a matter of doing the needful and meaningful thing at the appropriate time.

There have been times that I've had doctor's appointments scheduled. Upon making the appointment, I was made aware that I needed to show up at least fifteen minutes prior to the appointment time to fill out paperwork or obtain vital signs. The day prior to the appointment, I get a courtesy call reminding me of the appointment. Please tell me, how in the world do I wind up almost ten minutes late? To this day, that baffles me! Well, I'll tell you how it happens. It happens because I piddle around – procrastinating - getting my clothes out the night before and preparing, taking my shower, checking Facebook – as if something on there is beneficial or more important than my doctor's appointment - talking on the phone and doing all other kinds of nonsense rather than getting ready and leaving in a timely manner to get to the appointment on time. I waste all that "good gas" driving to the appointment, only to have someone tell me, "Sorry Mrs. Taylor, we are going to have to reschedule you." *Ugh!* Now whose fault is it? *Nobody's fault but my own.* And if it's happened to you, *nobody's fault but yours!* I have heard a saying that "prior proper planning prevents poor performance." That is a mindset change for the habitual procrastinator!

Let's take a look in the word of God at ten women – Wise and Foolish Virgins

> *"1 Then shall the kingdom of heaven be likened unto ten virgins, which took their lamps and went forth to meet their bridegroom.*

2 And five of them were wise, and five were foolish.

3 They that were foolish took their lamps and took no oil with them;

4 But the wise took oil in their vessels with their lamps.

5 While the bridegroom tarried, they all slumbered and slept.

6 And at midnight there was a cry made. Behold, the bridegroom cometh; go yet out to meet him.

7 Then all those virgins arose, and trimmed their lamps.

8 And the foolish said unto the wise, give us of your oil; for our lamps are gone out.

9 But the wise answered saying, NOT SO; lest there be not enough for us and you; but go ye rather to them that sell, and buy for yourselves.

10 And while they went to buy, the bridegroom came; and they that were ready went in with him to the marriage: and the door was shut.

11 Afterward came also the other virgins, saying, Lord, Lord, open to us.

12 But He answered and said, Verily I say unto you, I know you not.

13 Watch therefore, for ye know neither the day nor the hour wherein the Son of man cometh." Matthew 25: 1-13 (KJV)

We see here a lack of preparation on the behalf of the five foolish virgins. Their act of not preparing cost them an invitation to go into the wedding with the bridegroom. But there is so much more that's here. In the Word of God the previous chapter of Matthew, chapter 24 speaks to postponing preparation for the return of Jesus. However, in chapter 25, we see that the five wise virgins were prepared but the five foolish were not. It's interesting to me that this story didn't say three of the wise virgins had two foolish ones that hung out with them. It brings to mind the old adage "birds of a feather, flock together." The point I'm trying to make is, oftentimes, those that are ill prepared or procrastinate, have a tendency to hang around others that function the same way that they do. Those that are diligent and focused on trying to be prepared usually gravitate toward having the same type of people in their inner circle of friends - people to express themselves to. Likewise with those who are foolish, when you find a group of foolish women, if you look hard enough, you will see that the company that they keep also runs deep in the area of foolishness.

I have discovered that there is a fine line between procrastination and laziness. When you begin to examine what you *choose to do* over and above the thing that you *are supposed to be doing* you will discover *sleep* plays a large role in why you don't get certain things done in a timely manner. Even in the above parable, you see where *everyone went to sleep*, the wise virgins and the foolish. However, what stands out to me is how we can know that there is something we need to do or should have done, but we sleep on it anyway; we know that the work we have to do is yet to be done...*yet we are sleeping!*

Waiting until the last minute pushes us to a place I like to refer to as "RUSH HOUR!" Now typically, "rush hour" is a time of day whereby a large number of people are in transit, going to or returning from work, and that is characterized by particularly heavy traffic." (dictionary.com) However, "rush hour" for the procrastinator is just a tad bit different. For the person that has put things off until the last minute, rush hour becomes the hour, minutes, seconds prior to a due date or timeline for completion. During this time, adrenaline is flowing at its peak; your thoughts are racing to make sure you have covered every base there is. You're tracing and retracing your steps to make sure you have everything you need and that you didn't forget anything. You are trying to anticipate all avenues to ensure that you get it right the first time around. And because you've waited until the last minute, not only is it the first time around – it's actually the *last and only time around*! It's really crazy, because the procrastinator does not anticipate glitches or setbacks. The procrastinator does not consider room for error, because in the mind of the procrastinator *"this is going to be error free!"* What a farce!!!

Can I help you out? When you wait to the last minute, very rarely is it ever error free! There are always frequent mistakes and missed or overlooked information and details. The quality of the work is lacking, to say the least.

In the mind of a procrastinator, when we have waited until the last minute and there is a project involved, by the time we turn it in we honestly believe we are turning in a *masterpiece that is error free!* No joke! We don't prepare for catastrophes because we don't anticipate any. There's no need for all of that. Just take my completed project, check the block that says it's been submitted on time at the deadline and be grateful that it's not late! I'm telling you.... it is a mindset like none other.

Most of the people that I know that are procrastinators are not all that organized. In fact, it's just the opposite. We give the illusion of being organized, but in all actuality we have stuff all over the place. It may appear like a nice neat pile, but the truth is, we can't tell you where everything is, because honestly we don't know! Time management is the solution, but it is NOT our friend. Why? (I just love it when you ask why!) Well, truth is, we use our time wisely doing the things that we'd rather do. So, in the mind of the procrastinator, we have managed our time. Once again, we just haven't done the needful thing.

It's not funny, but what comes to mind are the number of planners that I buy during the course of one year. Other friends of mine that are procrastinators have that same little nasty habit. They purchase all types of planners, download the neatest apps on their phones to assist them with planning out their day, week, month and year. The only problem is they don't stick to those plans. None of us do; we do the stuff that is more relevant, in our eyes, to our lives. That brings me to the next thing we need to tackle; and it's called *selfishness*.

Someone recently asked me "why does a procrastinator get upset when they are left behind if car pooling when their last minute shenanigans would cause others to be late?" My response to that is very simple. Most procrastinators never really expect their habit or behavior to be called on the carpet and addressed by anyone. So, actually creating a scenario where a procrastinator has to suffer the consequences of his or her own actions, forces the procrastinator to either take a good look in the mirror or present an excuse that would make the procrastinator look or feel like a victim.

You see, in today's society, there are a lot of people that have upper level management positions. That doesn't always mean that they have good management or people skills. The individual may have the skill set needed to do a particular job well but when dealing with people, you must factor in that everyone does not respond to similar situations in the same manner. Therefore, confronting habits and behaviors such as procrastination doesn't always get addressed. So many people choose to be non-confrontational. Rather than addressing an individual's area of weakness, many choose to just let it slide and keep the peace. This goes back to the "enabler."

Scripture declares that *"And you will know the truth, and the truth will set you free." John 8: 32 (NLT)* When truth shines a light on an individual and makes them aware that they need to change it's not always pleasant. Not everyone appreciates, embraces or likes change. In fact, it's just the opposite. When a person's negative traits are confronted, it seems as if the tendency is to cast blame or deny that the negative trait exists.

Change does not take place when things are
not addressed.

Please hear me on this! If you avoid addressing issues of procrastination or any other issue, for that matter, I can almost guarantee you that nothing will change for a significant amount of time. You can't expect change if you *never address the issue*! Passing the buck and beating around the bush just doesn't cut it! For the procrastinator – truth works in our lives! So when the truth of God's word speaks and lets us know that it's time to establish some new habits, and it's time to make some changes, please know that God is trying to set us free!

Note(s) to self from this chapter

_____
_____
_____
_____
_____
_____
_____
_____
_____
_____
_____
_____

Write your own personal daily affirmations

_____
_____
_____
_____
_____
_____
_____
_____
_____
_____
_____
_____

CHAPTER FIVE

The *Fun* Factor

I'm going to let you in on a little secret. Most procrastinators enjoy the spontaneity of things that are laced with pleasure - fun! Seriously, if all tasks that needed to be completed were surrounded by something of "our particular area of interest" then we wouldn't be so apt to put it off. These are a few of the things *I know for a fact that we do when we want to avoid doing what needs to be done.*

We do absolutely *Nothing* – (idleness)! We waste a lot of time daydreaming about the things we would rather be doing. We focus on *"Tomorrow"* and what all we can get accomplished on the next day.

Objective
Explain what procrastinators are really doing when they aren't doing what they're supposed to do

I'm going to share another transparent moment with you. In the introduction, I shared with you about the dream job I had. I also shared how it quickly became the 'Nightmare on Job Street' too. There were just piles and piles of work that I could never get accomplished on time. Prior to my leaving the job, I remember the Lord birthing in me the need to write this book. I was burdened to write for a few reasons - 1: to help myself; and 2 – to, prayerfully, help others. So, the first thing I did was begin to interview different co-workers, family, church family and friends. I also did quite a bit of research on the topic of procrastination. But what began to happen was God began to give me revelation on my actions.

One of the things I noticed was what I would do when I was extremely fatigued and I knew that I had a deadline to meet. I found myself calculating the number of hours it would take me to complete the task I had ahead of me. I would calculate the amount of time I could sleep and subtract it from the number of hours I had left before I needed to report to work. Procrastination isn't about time, because on the clock of a procrastinator, you get around to it when it's convenient for you. *That's Really A Glorified Form Of Selfishness.* Remember these words from chapter one? They give a general description of our attitude concerning tasks that we *need* to be performing. However, when there is nothing fun or pleasurable about the task needing to be accomplished then we have a tendency to operate using one of the methods listed in the glossary below until it is either convenient or detrimental.

Block   Put on the back burner

Delay   Put on hold

Detain   Put on ice

Extend	Set aside
Give rain check	Shelve
Hold up	Stall
Impede	Slow
Lay over	Suspend
Lengthen	Table
Postpone	Wave

It's needful that you understand that in the mind of a person that has not overcome procrastination, the average thought process doesn't involve anyone but the procrastinator. The very clock that we operate by indicates an abstract time of "whenever" – whenever it is convenient for us to complete the task is about the time we will attempt to complete it. Most of the time there is no one else on our minds. We are truly processing from a place of "me, myself and I." We are asking ourselves questions like: "How long will this take? What kind of short cut can I take? How much do I really need to do?" We also assess what we can do to make it look as if we've worked long and hard on the project so that it reflects that we have really done an outstanding job.

Not one time do we consider that something could go wrong to hinder our little, devised plan. We dare not factor in any computer issues, auditing problems, errors or otherwise. What's even crazier is our level of expectation. We expect people to be in place to cater to our "last minuteness or lateness!" Isn't that absurd? But it is the truth. There is that sense of entitlement we feel, especially when it was aided by someone in our lives who enabled us along the way, thinking everyone must conform to our revised production schedule and altered timeline. Without the accountability to stay on schedule, we stay that much further off task. Even with accountability, when procrastination is a stronghold, it remains a battle to be disciplined enough to complete a task in a timely manner.

From the interviews I conducted, most people had no clue as to why they waited until the last minute to complete a task. The things that they did with their time were not fruitful in most instances, it was just time wasted… watching TV, social media, talking on the phone. Once again, idleness and selfishness are seen at work.

What does the word say about being idle?

Here is something that is worth repeating - Holy Spirit revealed it to me this way:

"Lazy can; but won't. Procrastination does; but later, eventually."

From a spiritual perspective, there are extremes to almost everything. There is a vast difference between procrastination and laziness. However, when the habits of a procrastinator begin to incorporate more sleep in their pattern than simply working on another project, now they're positioning themselves for a spirit of laziness to oppress them.

Procrastination and laziness can affect a person's well being, relationships, performance and health. They can also lead to grave regret. We can't go back and reclaim days, weeks, months, years. When we procrastinate, we risk excellence, thus possibly ruining relationships with clients, customers or associates. It can ruin our reputation. A good name is better to be had than silver and gold. As children of God, we should be concerned about our reputations. We should strive to walk in excellence in all that we do.

Everything we do, we should do it as unto God, pleasing Him. *Colossians 3:23-24 (NLT) tells us," Work willingly at whatever you do, as though you were working for the Lord rather than for people. Remember that the Lord will give you an inheritance as your reward, and that the Master you are serving is Christ."*

Note(s) to self from this chapter

_____
_____
_____
_____
_____
_____
_____
_____
_____
_____
_____
_____

Write your own personal daily affirmations

_____
_____
_____
_____
_____
_____
_____
_____
_____
_____
_____
_____

CHAPTER SIX

Your *Health*

Right before resigning from my previous job, I experienced a grave health scare. I was going about my everyday life working, putting things off per my norm, continuing to do the series of things that I was doing in conjunction with my job. On one particular morning I noticed that I was out of my blood pressure medication. So I made a call to reorder the medication. While I was on hold, I decided to take my BP and at the time I took it, it registered 212/120. I thought to myself...."this machine must be defective." Now mind you, the device was brand new. Well, you know what I did? I packed it up and returned it to the store and got another one. This time it was a little more expensive and, in my mind, a tad better quality than the one I returned. It was approximately an hour and a half in between the purchase

Objective
Provide you with the hidden effects of stress. This chapter is designed to make you aware of what stress induces mentally, physically, emotionally and spiritually

of the new device and when I had last taken my blood pressure. I got back home and retook my BP. This time it read 218/ 126. Again I thought to myself... "Why is this store selling all of these defective devices?" Guess what I did after that? I packed that one up and mailed it off to my mother. By this point, although I was in denial, I had a feeling my BP might be running a bit high; I just didn't know "how high." I went back to the store one final time and purchased the best BP device the store had. It was a name brand device and was a bit on the expensive side in terms of cost. I didn't take my BP right away. I went and picked up my BP medication. I took the medication and waited about thirty minutes or so and opened up my new machine. By now it was several hours later than when I took it the last time. This time the reading was 232/148! You know I went through my little ritual and made the assessment that the device was defective. So instead of returning the device, I went to a local pharmacy and took my blood pressure with their machine. To my surprise, the reading was the same 232/148! I contacted my provider and was instructed to go immediately to the hospital. I fussed a little bit about it and tried to give a little resistance, but the handwriting was on the wall. My pressure had been creeping up all day.

I don't like hospitals and all of that. Although I am a nurse by profession, I don't like being sick and I am NOT a good patient. While lying in the emergency room, I began to reflect on things concerning my body. I was lying there thinking about how I had been feeling all that month and days leading up to the ER visit. I was not getting enough sleep or rest due to staying up all night trying to finish things that should have already been done. I was thinking about the physical signs and symptoms I was having but refused to share with anyone. I was literally experiencing tingling in my face, and it seemed as though when I would smile, there was numbness on one side of my face. I was fearful that I was having a stroke - I really was. I didn't share it with anyone at all because, in my mind, it was all a trick of the enemy. What stands out the most to me is the fact that I was receiving a download about the topic of procrastination.

I began to pay close attention to the things I was doing at the last minute, how I was feeling, thoughts I was processing and making the connection to the spirit of procrastination. It began to dawn on me that the enemy of my soul was truly after me to kill me. He was using my habit of putting things off to induce the physical stress that comes with "pressure and uncertainty" to incite an infirmity and condition. It was designed to keep me from completing an ultimate assignment - primarily the completion of this book.

> *The thief cometh not but for to steal, kill and destroy. John 10:10(KJV)*

> *"The thief's purpose is to steal and kill and destroy. My purpose is to give life in all its fullness." John 10: 10 (NLT)*

We have quoted that scripture time and time again. I don't add anything to the word of God or take anything away from it. However, I like to point out a game changer when quoting that scripture. Quote that scripture and point at yourself at the end and say "ME". That is a game changer. Prior to doing that, I knew that the word of God applied to me. Yet, when I would quote that scripture, it didn't resonate in my spirit until I made it more up close and personal by saying the word "me!" It immediately made me more cognizant of the fact that the devil hates me and he's out to destroy me by any means necessary.

So, while at that so called dream job, I began to notice with each passing day, as the pressures would mound for me to get certain things completed – knowing that I was already behind - I began to notice physical changes in my body. On several occasions, I felt a tingling in my face. I would have frequent headaches. My blood pressure was over the roof. It was beyond crazy. I was gaining weight at an out-of-control rate. I ate constantly, in large part, due to stress; but I continued to press forward, trying to hang in there.

I positioned myself for increased stress as I refused to ask anyone for help when I was in over my head. Now, that may not be true for all or even most procrastinators. Some may do a better job at tapping into the help or expertise around them to pull things together at the last minute. However, the one thing I was pretty horrible at doing was calling for someone to help me or assist me in getting caught up with my work.

Here's the revelation as it pertains to your health. Earlier in the book I asked you to assess yourself, to think back to the earliest time you can remember putting things off. As I interviewed different people to collect information for this book, I found that procrastination did not discriminate. There was no one particular demographic that was targeted regarding the habit of procrastination. However, what I discovered was the limitation and toll that procrastination begins to take on you as you age.

What do I mean by that? Glad you asked! If you are reading this and you are relatively young, let's say in your teens all the way up to your thirties even, well, it seems like a piece of cake to put things off and wait until the last second, organize in your mind how to tackle the project, do a couple of all nighters and then "get 'er done." The problem is, as you age, the truth of the matter is, you just don't function as quickly as you once did. Seriously, your mind tells you 'I can get all of this stuff done in a few minutes or a couple of hours.' But the fact is you can't.

> *"I tell you the truth, when you were young, you were able to do as you liked; you dressed yourself and went wherever you wanted to go. But when you are old, you will stretch out your hands, and others will dress you and take you where you don't want to go." John 21: 18 (NLT)*

I can already hear a religious demon knocking on the portals of your mind quoting the scripture: *"I can do all things through Christ who gives me strength." Philippians 4: 13 (KJV)*. I know that with God all things are possible, but do you realize how fast you used to run when you were younger, or how long you could play outside all day without getting tired? The enemy of our souls wants us to disregard our physical limitations. We were not built to stay under constant pressure and stress. Ultimately, when we continue the practice of putting things off until the last minute that are of importance or perhaps are tied into our livelihood, we position ourselves for an attack on our physical bodies.

Indeed, stress symptoms can affect your body, your thoughts and feelings, and your behavior. Being able to recognize common stress symptoms can give you a jump on managing them. Stress that's left unchecked can contribute toward many health problems, such as high blood pressure, heart disease, obesity and diabetes.

Stress symptoms: Effects on your body and behavior - Mayo Clinic

The enemy doesn't want to be exposed in this manner or light. He wants us to continue in the vein of putting things off and then rushing to get it done, thus putting us at risk for destruction and death. When we operate like this, we are only being set up for an eventual downfall.

ANXIETY – Worry, apprehension, dread, fear, nervousness, panic, restlessness, uneasiness, tension, fretfulness

STRESS – Tension, worry, anxiety, mental breakdown, nervous breakdown, stroke, strain" (Demon Hit List, John Eckhardt)

For more information on the effects of stress please go check out *www.mayoclinic.org/healthy-lifestyle/stress.../in.../stress.../art-2005098*

Here's the vicious cycle:

Project introduced → Deadline given →

Expectations verbalized & more often than not – understood

Procrastinators start out with the best intentions of completing the project in a timely fashion → Attention diverted to something else that is more suitable or pleasurable →

Project put on hold

Others that have the same or similar assignments are completing their assigned task →

Excuses begin to show up

Note(s) to self from this chapter

_____
_____
_____
_____
_____
_____
_____
_____
_____
_____
_____
_____

Write your own personal daily affirmations

_____
_____
_____
_____
_____
_____
_____
_____
_____
_____
_____
_____

CHAPTER SEVEN

Devices *and* Strategies

"Lest Satan should get an advantage of us: for we are not ignorant of his devices." 2 Corinthians 2:11 (KJV)

Objective

To release game-changing information and insights to expose the plan of the enemy which is to steal, kill and destroy YOU; To share the enemy's ultimate purpose and reveal his plan to prevent you from accepting Jesus and ultimately deny you the opportunity to serve God

Up until now, I've taken you through the profile of a procrastinator. I've tried to enhance the knowledge of those of you that may encounter a procrastinator so that you will know exactly what you are dealing with. If you are a procrastinator and you are reading this book, then the objective was to let you see that you are not alone in your struggle, but the time is at hand for you to do something about this little nagging, nasty, underestimated habit.

"Behold, I send you forth as sheep in the midst of wolves; be ye therefore wise as

75

*serpents, and harmless as doves." Matthew
10: 16 (KJV)*

You see, it is one thing to put off doing a paper, completing an assignment, finishing chores, paying a bill or being on time for an appointment. But it is an entirely different ball game when you are talking about a *kingdom appointment* and delaying the purposes and plans of God.

I've touched on what happens hypothetically when we miss appointments, interviews, etc. as a result of procrastination. Now we need to address postponing moving on the word of God and its detrimental implications for the Body of Christ and the world.

When we buy-in to the lie that we can do things later, because it is a mindset, we tend to not discriminate. It's amazing to me how the enemy will get us to twist scripture for his cause. Again, I can hear how the enemy of our soul will scream out to us at the most inopportune time "You can do all things through Christ which strengthens you!" Philippians 4: 13 (KJV) The devil wants us to feel that we can live right...*later*. We can repent...*later*. We can forgive... *later*. Remember, putting off what needs to happen now until later is a stronghold, a developed habit - a mindset.

There are tons of studies out there that give a time frame of how long it takes to establish a habit. Recent research led by a team at the University College London think they have uncovered just how long (on average) it takes for something to become habitual. They do not think it takes twenty-one days to form a habit. They believe it takes an average of sixty-six days to create a habit.

How Long Does it Take to Form A Habit?

Many are called but few are chosen. (Matthew 22:14). When God has chosen us for a thing – a cause, a purpose, an assignment - there is no point in putting it off.

It is imperative that we understand that God has blessed us with so many things - gifts, talents, resources – to include finances, intelligence, positions, opportunities and more. He expects us to put them to use to bring glory to His name. He expects us to be good stewards over that which He has entrusted us. He doesn't want us to bury or hide anything that He has given us. He wants to see us wisely use our time and talents and *not wait until the last minute*. He does not want us come up with some cockamamie excuse that makes absolutely no sense in order to justify our lack of judgment with the use of time and opportunities we've been given in order to get something of worth or value completed.

> *"For it is just like a man going on a journey. He called his own slaves and turned over his possessions to them. To one he gave five talents; to another, two; and to another, one – to each according to his own ability. Then he went on a journey. Immediately the man who had received five talents went, put them to work, and earned five more. In the same way the man with two earned two more. But*

77

the man who had received one talent went off, dug a hole in the ground, and hid his master's money. After a long time the master of those slaves came and settled accounts with them. The man who had received five talents approached, presented five more talents, and said, 'Master, you gave me five talents. Look, I've earned five more talents.' His master said to him, 'Well done, good and faithful slave! You were faithful over a few things; I will put you in charge of many things. Share your master's joy!' Then the man with two talents also approached. He said, 'Master, you gave me two talents. Look, I've earned two more talents.' His master said to him, 'Well done, good and faithful slave! You were faithful over a few things; I will put you in charge of many things. Share your master's joy! Then the man who had received one talent also approached and said, 'Master, I know you. You're a difficult man, reaping where you haven't sown and gathering where you haven't scattered seed. So I was afraid and went off and hid your talent in the ground. Look you have what is yours. But his master replied to him, 'you evil, lazy slave! If you knew that I reap where I haven't sown and gather where I haven't scattered, then you should have deposited my money with the bankers. And when I returned I would have received my money back with interest. So take the talent from him and give it to the one who has 10 talents. For to everyone who has, more will be given, and he will have more than enough. But from the one who does not have, even what he has will be taken away from him. And throw this good-for-nothing slave into the outer darkness. In that place there will be weeping and gnashing of teeth." Matthew 25:14-30 (HSB)

The enemy of our soul knows that his time is limited. Therefore, he uses the one thing that we take for granted to take advantage of us.. Satan wants us to believe that we have all the time in the world, that we are invincible. It's easy to feel as though you are going to live forever – especially when you are young. You feel as though you have a lifetime to get your act together. But in all actuality, you don't.

Although this parable has nothing to do with age, it does portray the fact that we put off the things of God in order to pursue or follow after the things of the world.

"When one of those who reclined at the table with Him heard these things, he said to Him, 'The one who will eat bread in the kingdom of God is blessed?' Then He told him: 'A man was giving a large banquet and invited many. At the time of the banquet, he

*sent his slave to tell those who were invited,
'Come, because everything is now ready.'
But without exception they all began to
make excuses. The first one said to him, I
have bought a field, and I must go out and
see it. I ask you to excuse me. Another said,
'I have bought five yoke of oxen, and I'm
going to try them out. I ask you to excuse
me.' And another said, 'I just got married,
and therefore I'm unable to come.' So the
slave came back and reported these things
to his master. Then in anger, the master of
the house told his slave, 'Go out quickly into
the streets and alleys of the city, and bring
in here the poor, maimed, blind, and lame!'
'Master, the slave said, 'what you ordered
has been done, and there's still room.'
'Then the master told the slave, 'Go out into
the highways and lanes and make them
come in, so that my house may be filled. For
I tell you, not one of those men who were
invited will enjoy my banquet!" Luke 14:
15-24 (KJV)*

When we put things off, let the record show, we are
aligning ourselves with what scripture declares as one that
is "wicked, evil, and lazy." There are consequences and
repercussions; not only is that the case in the natural, but
even more so in the spiritual realm.

In conferring with a non-procrastinator, I was informed how it makes their skin crawl when working with people who wait to the last minute to get things done. I felt like that was a bit extreme, but at the same token, our behaviors don't bother US. They bother YOU. We generally don't get all worked up and in a frenzy because of the opinions of others. Here's the revelation though.... If you truly check this area of your life, it's an area that you have *not surrendered to Christ!*

When we refuse to surrender areas to Christ that we know need adjusting, it is indeed a sin. Growth and maturity in the word of God point in the direction of change and transformation. As we grow in the word, there will be areas that we will be convicted of that require our attention - attention to change! The word of God is a love letter to us with a clarion call that will aid us in transforming to become all that God desires us to be.

> *"Therefore, ridding yourselves of all moral filth and evil, humbly receive the implanted word, which is able to save you. But be doers of the word and not hearers only, deceiving yourselves. Because if anyone is a hearer of the word and not a doer, he is like a man looking at his own face in a mirror. For he looks at himself, goes away, and immediately forgets what kind of man he was. But the one who looks intently into the perfect law of freedom and perseveres in it,*

81

and is not a forgetful hearer but one who does good works - this person will be blessed in what he does." James 1: 21–25 (HSB)

Spending time in the word, in prayer and allowing the Spirit of God to love on us and groom us for greater is the recipe for growth and maturity in every area of our lives. It's the little foxes that spoil the vine. In other words, it's those small issues that we don't like to address that create some of the largest issues in our lives. When we discipline ourselves to get in the Word of God, we begin to see the specks in our eyes that we need to deal with. I've said it before and I believe it's worth repeating: you may feel as though you have functioned at the highest peak of your game being a procrastinator, but the devil has *beguiled you.*

"I beseech you therefore, brethren, by the mercies of God, that ye present your bodies a living sacrifice, holy, acceptable unto God, which is your reasonable service. And be not conformed to this world: but be ye transformed by the renewing of your mind that ye may prove what is that good and acceptable, and perfect will of God." Romans 12: 1, 2 (KJV)

Here is a revelation that you are not even ready for.... at least I know I wasn't. Check out this scripture:

"Come now, you who say 'Today or tomorrow we will travel to such and such a city and spend a year there and do business and make a profit.' You don't even know what tomorrow will bring – what your life will be! For you are like smoke that appears for a little while, then vanishes. Instead, you should say, 'If the Lord wills, we will live and do this or that.' But as it is, you boast in your arrogance. All such boasting is evil. So it is a sin for the person who knows to do what is good and doesn't do it." James 4:13-17 (HSB)

Please review

*examinedexistence.com/how-**long-does-it-take**-for-something-to-become-a-**habit**/*

for more information on habit formation.

Note(s) to self from this chapter

_____
_____
_____
_____
_____
_____
_____
_____
_____
_____
_____

Write your own personal daily affirmations

_____
_____
_____
_____
_____
_____
_____
_____
_____
_____
_____
_____

Setting *a* Kingdom Standard

"Commit thy works unto the Lord, and thy thoughts shall be established."

Proverbs 16: 3 (KJV)

There is so, so much in this scripture

"Servants, obey in all things your masters according to the flesh; not with eyeservice, as menpleasers ; but in singleness of heart, fearing God. And whatsoever ye do, do it heartily, as to the Lord, and not unto men; Knowing that of the Lord ye shall receive the reward of the inheritance: for ye serve the Lord Christ. But he that doeth wrong shall receive for the wrong which he hath done; and there is no respect of persons."
Colossians 3:21–25 (KJV)

"Servants, do what you're told by your earthly masters. And don't just do the minimum that will get you by. Do your best. Work from the heart for your real Master, for God, confident that you'll get paid in full when you come into your inheritance. Keep in mind always that the ultimate Master you're serving is Christ. The sullen servant who does shoddy work will be held responsible. Being a follower of Jesus doesn't cover up bad work." Colossians 3:21–25 (MSG)

Wow! Did you see that? "Being a follower of Jesus doesn't cover up bad work." Ijs.

Objective

To show that Excellence is associated with the Kingdom of God, along with love, peace, righteousness, and joy in the Holy Ghost

I want you to see this in different versions so you can glean all that Father will allow you to see. First of all when we procrastinate – put things off until the last minute, I'm convinced that it is not our *best work*. In fact, it is our *rushed work*! It's not like we have any time left to see if we could have done any better because we have *lost all of the time we have to try and do anything better!* All we have is all we have! You deprive yourself of even knowing if you could have given anything better than what you had to offer, if you hadn't waited until the last minute.

Secondly, this scripture uses a word in the Message Bible that I just love... *'minimum.'* It says 'don't just do the minimum.' It categorizes the work we offer as just enough to get by. Listen to me and hear me well. When you can bypass check points and enter into something where you are *rushing* because you've waited until the last minute, that automatically lets me know that the category we are dealing with is the minimum category. You see, when we rush, there is a tendency to make mistakes and miss small things. We don't pay as close attention to detail as we should or that we would, if we were taking advantage of our time.

When we are functioning in a Kingdom mindset, we have a revelation and insight of "rewards!" Hallelujah! We know that there is more to life than what is right here on earth. Not only that, we recognize that we may be able to get over on people, but we cannot get over on God. He sees our actions and the intent of our actions.

Here's the crazy thing, when we work diligently as unto Him, He is so gracious, He will reward us even here on earth.

In Chapter One of this book, I suggested that you do a self-assessment as it pertains to procrastination. One of the questions I asked you to examine was *"are you ready for a change?"* To the average person that may not be prone to procrastinating, the question may seem a tad rhetorical. However, to the procrastinator, the question truly requires a thought-provoking reply. It requires us to look deep within ourselves and make a determination as to whether or not we want to continue on with life as usual or take small steps toward developing a Kingdom Mindset and performing Kingdom Actions.

When referring to the Kingdom, I'm referring to the Kingdom of God!

> *"Let not your good be evil spoken of: For the kingdom of God is not meat and drink; but righteousness, and peace, and joy in the Holy Ghost. For he that in these things serveth Christ is acceptable to God, and approved of men. Let us therefore follow after the things which make for peace, and things wherewith one may edify another."* *Romans 14: 16-19 (KJV)*

> *"For the Kingdom of God is not a matter of what we eat or drink, but of living a life of goodness and peace and joy in the Holy Spirit." Romans 14: 17 (NLT)*

I really like how the Amplified Bible breaks down this scripture: *"If your brother is being hurt or offended because of food {toward him}. Do not let what you are eating destroy and spiritually harm one for whom Christ died. Therefore do not let what is a good thing for you {because of your freedom to choose} be spoken of as evil {by someone else}; for the kingdom of God is not a matter of eating and drinking {what one likes}, but of righteousness and peace and joy in the Holy Spirit. For the one who serves Christ in this way {recognizing that food choice is secondary] is acceptable to God and is approved by men. So then, let us pursue {with enthusiasm} the things which make for peace and the building up of one another {things which lead to spiritual growth}." Romans 14: 15–19 (AMP)*

"Run from anything that stimulates youthful lusts. Instead, pursue righteous living, faithfulness, love and peace. Enjoy the companionship of those who call on the Lord with pure hearts." 2 Timothy 2:22 (NLT)

If we are going to win over the world and be a representative of Christ in the earth realm, we must operate in excellence. There is nothing excellent about waiting until the last minute or being late all the time. Kingdom-minded people *set and keep a standard for excellence.* Some may strongly dislike you because you set a higher standard. When you operate in excellence, there will be those that rise up against you because you represent Christ. The Lord encourages us that our gift will make room for us and bring us before kings as long as we do everything as unto the Lord.

We have to remember to sow seeds of production and not of idleness and slothfulness when operating in the Kingdom of God. God's vision and plans will come to pass whether we choose to be obedient or not, but who would want to miss the call of God because of a negative mindset?

> *"Be not deceived; God is not mocked: for whatsoever a man soweth, that shall he also reap." Galatians 6:7*

When you sow seeds of doing things at the last minute then you begin to create a name for yourself as a person whom cannot be trusted to operate in excellence. Having a Kingdom mindset and setting Kingdom standards involve your heart. There comes a time that as we grow and mature in the word of God, we want to please the Father above all else. We shouldn't want to just keep doing things our own way – mediocre or 'just enough to get by.' We should want to please the Father with our thoughts, words, and deeds and transition to not just good but great.

I intentionally wanted to establish for you that there is a difference between laziness and procrastination.

Dealing With Daniel – The Spirit of Excellence

Excellent

1. Possessing outstanding quality or superior merit, remarkably good.

2. Archaic. Extraordinary, superior.

Let's take a look at the book of Daniel and see what the Word of God has to declare regarding excellence.

> *"Forasmuch as an excellent spirit, and knowledge, and understanding, interpreting of dreams, and shewing of hard sentences, and dissolving of doubts, were found in the same Daniel, whom the king named Beleshazzar; now let Daniel be called, and he will shew the interpretation." Daniel 5: 12 (KJV)*

> *"I have even heard of thee, that the spirit of the gods is in thee, and that light and understanding and excellent wisdom is found in thee." Daniel 5: 14 (KJV)*

> *"Then this Daniel was preferred above the presidents and princes, because an excellent spirit was in him; and the king thought to set him over the whole realm." Daniel 6: 3 (KJV)*

Daniel displayed a spirit of excellence. When referring to the Kingdom of God, the God of the Most High, surely thoughts of procrastination, laziness, lethargy, sluggish, slothful, complacent, late, tardy – cannot be what comes to your mind. Quite the contrary! *Excellence is synonymous with the god of our salvation. "The Lord is not slack concerning his promise, as some men count slackness; but is longsuffering to us-ward, not willing that any should perish, but that all should come to repentance."* 2 Peter 3: 9 (KJV).

Daniel was placed in a position of authority; he was placed as a "Prime Minister" so to speak, because of his diligence. Diligence paves the way to open doors of opportunity. Diligence paves the way for reward - both with man and with God. Diligence sets you apart from the mundane and complacent. Diligence is synonymous with a godly kingdom mindset. As a kingdom representative, the mindset, work ethic and effort to accomplish a task assigned involves our being consistently attentive and persistent to the task until it is completed; *not waiting until the last minute, throwing something together on a hope and a prayer* using the cliché "I do my best work under pressure." That is truly *not* of God. In fact, that is a carnal *excuse* for why the flesh did not tackle a project or an assignment using the time allotted wisely.

Diligent

1. Constant in effort to accomplish something; attentive and persistent in doing anything.

2. Done or pursued with persevering attention; painstaking:

Diligence – the constant and earnest effort to accomplish what is undertaken; persistent exertion of body or mind.

SCRIPTURES:

> *"The hand of the diligent shall bear rule: but the slothful shall be under tribute."*
> *Proverbs 12: 24 (KJV)*

> *"The hand of the diligent will rule, but the negligent and lazy will be put to forced labor." Proverbs 12: 24 (AMP)*

> *"Be thou diligent to know the state of thy flocks, and look well to thy herds."*
> *Proverbs 27: 23 (KJV)*

"And we have sent with them our brother, whom we have oftentimes proved diligent in many things, but now much more diligent, upon the great confidence which I have in you." 2 Corinthians 8: 22 (KJV)

"We have sent with them our brother, whom we have often tested and found to be diligent in many things, but who is now even more diligent {than ever} because of his great confidence in you." 2 Corinthians 8:22 (AMP)

"He becometh poor that dealeth with a slack hand: but the hand of the diligent maketh rich." Proverbs 10:4 (KJV)

"Poor is he that works with a negligent and idle hand, but the hand of the diligent makes him rich." Proverbs 10:4 (AMP)

"The soul of the sluggard desireth, and hath nothing; but the soul of the diligent shall be made fat." Proverbs 13:4 (KJV)

"The soul (appetite) of the lazy person craves and gets nothing {for lethargy overcomes ambition}, But the soul (appetite) of the diligent {who works willingly} is rich and abundantly supplied." Proverbs 13:4 (AMP)

"The thoughts of the diligent tend only to plenteousness; but of every one that is hasty only to want." Proverbs 21: 5 (KJV)

"Thou hast commanded us to keep thy precepts diligently." Psalms 119: 4 (KJV)

"Or he that exhorteth, on exhortation; he that giveth, let him do it with simplicity; he that ruleth, with diligence; he that sheweth mercy with cheerfulness." Romans 12: 8 (KJV)

"But without faith it is impossible to please him: for he that cometh to God must believe that he is, and that he is a rewarder of them that diligently seek him." Hebrews 11: 6 (KJV)

"Therefore, as ye abound in everything, in faith, and utterance, and knowledge, and in all diligence, and in our love to us, see that ye abound in this grace also."

2 Corinthians 8: 7 (KJV)

Look at this scripture. Examine the prerequisites in order for a widow to receive assistance or help of any kind:

"A widow is to be put on the list (to receive regular assistance) only if she is over sixty years of age, (having been) the wife of one man, and has a reputation for good deeds; (she is eligible) if she has brought up children, if she has shown hospitality to strangers, if she has washed the feet of the saints (God's people), if she has assisted the distressed, and had devoted herself to doing good in every way." 1 Timothy 5: 9-10 (AMP) (bold lettering mine)

"Well reported of for good works; if she have brought up children, if she have lodged strangers, if she have washed the saints' feet, if she have relieved the afflicted, if she have diligently followed every good work." 1 Timothy 5: 10 (KJV).

With anything that is done over time, I'm of the belief that if it is done well, your name will be heard of. In any area of business, education, sports/athletics, sales, custodial, fashion, financial, music, acting, dance, ministry etc. we position ourselves to gain a reputation. Reputations can be either good or bad. When we function diligently and in excellence as opposed to being an individual who postpones things until the last minute, we are now in a position to be considered to rule or be placed in charge.

However, the opposite holds true when you gain the reputation for being a last minute person or a slacker. Please remember that I shared with you earlier on in the book that all procrastinators are not lazy or slackers. The problem is, when you work with others and you are a procrastinator, *others are aware that you are a last minute kind of person.* Procrastination doesn't always discriminate. It will show up at some point and time and announce its presence. In other words, you may get by for years putting things off at the last minute... until one day someone will get a glimpse of your flaw. When that happens, just know you will be monitored closely to see if it was an isolated incident that occurred or if it is a habit that can create issues for you down the road.

When we are born, we arrive here on earth with somewhat of a clean slate as it pertains to our name. Some may be born into families that have stellar names or perhaps just the opposite is true. You may have been born into that family that is known for something that carries a negative connotation. However, I believe that we are all given the opportunity to individually *create the name we desire for ourselves.* From childhood, all the way up into our adult lives, opportunities are presented for us to put forth effort or participate in things. We start out with school, and on to a trade school or perhaps on to college, or possibly on to the military, or right into the work force – whatever the choice may be, many are starting to focus on future dreams and desires. If you look back in retrospect, you will find that you began to develop a name for yourself as it pertains to your work ethic, early on. If the reputation that you've acquired has been negative, does that mean you can't change? Of course not!! At some point and time, you just have to choose to do something about it, especially if you don't like it!

You have the power and the authority to do something about it! Greatness resides on the inside of you. *"Ye are of God, little children, and have overcome them: because greater is he that is in you, than he that is in the world." 1 John 4:4 (KJV)*

We have a choice! We can choose to have a good name or not to have a good name. It's really up to us! If we've acquired a poor reputation for doing things at the last minute or being late, etc. we are able to change that reputation by doing things differently. *No one may ever know that you wait until the last minute to do things required of you. But God knows.* A kingdom mindset will take the initiative to do a self-assessment and come to the conclusion that "consistently waiting until the last minute is not in line with a spirit of excellence, diligence or the

98

character of God." Once the light comes on in that area and you have an epiphany of all of which the enemy is trying to rob you, then I believe that you will make the necessary shift in your thought process and actions to rid yourself of this gripping stronghold and put forth the efforts toward change!

When we have a kingdom mindset, we should desire a good name, a good reputation!

> *"A good name (earned by honorable behavior, godly wisdom, moral courage, and personal integrity) is more desirable than great riches; and favor is better than silver and gold." Proverbs 22:1 (AMP)*

> *"Choose a good reputation over great riches; being held in high esteem is better than silver or gold." Proverbs 22:1 (NLT)*

> *"A sterling reputation is better than striking it rich; a gracious spirit is better than money in the bank." Proverbs 22:1 (MSG)*

> *"A good name is better than precious perfume. And the day of one's death better than the day of one's birth." Ecclesiastes 7:1 (AMP)*

> *"A good reputation is better than a fat bank account..." Ecclesiastes 7: 1a (MSG)*

"A good reputation is more valuable than costly perfume..." Ecclesiastes 7: 1a (NLT)

"A good name is better than precious ointment..." Ecclesiastes 7: 1a (KJV)

Please note that everyone may not like you. Everyone may not speak well of you. But when the facts are the facts, let people say what they will! Because when you are walking in excellence you will be sought after! When you are diligent it will show up in your work, in your labor of love. Father needs his children in key places and positions. He wants to entrust us that way. The people are happy when the righteous rule.

"When the righteous are in authority, the people rejoice: but when the wicked beareth rule, the people mourn." Proverbs 29:2 (KJV)

"When good people run things, everyone is glad, but when the ruler is bad, everyone groans." Proverbs 29:2 (MSG)

"When the righteous are in authority and become great, the people rejoice; but when

100

*the wicked man rules, the people groan and
sigh." Proverbs 29:2 (AMP)*

*"When the godly are in authority, the people
rejoice. But when the wicked are in power,
they groan." Proverbs 29:2 (NLT)*

Ultimately, as a kingdom minded believer, we are to
function independently on assignments entrusted to us by
Father, just like the ants. We have an assignment and our
ability to be disciplined and diligent go hand in hand. We
shouldn't have to have someone monitor or micromanage
us. There isn't a need for it when we are kingdom minded.
The end effect of our procrastination can be devastating.
When we do not see the error of our ways as it pertains to
putting things off, it can affect our positioning as it pertains
to finances.

*"Take a lesson from the ants, you lazy-
bones. Learn from their ways and be wise!
Even though they have no prince, governor,
or ruler to make them work, they labor hard
all summer, gathering food for the winter.
But you, lazybones, how long will you sleep,
a little more slumber, a little folding of the
hands to rest – poverty will pounce on you*

like a bandit; scarcity will attack you like an
armed robber." Prov. 6:6-11 (NLT)

Do you not realize that this scripture gives insights to a person that is "lazy"? However, one of the things that we don't pay attention to as a procrastinator is when we go from a place of procrastination and shift to a place of laziness. I was determined to make sure that I highlighted the correlation to sleep and laziness! It's imperative that we assess how we are spending our time. It's one thing to be doing other things and putting something off to the last minute. But it's an entirely different ballgame when we are wasting that time *sleeping*!

Either way it goes laziness nor
procrastination have any place in the setting
of a Kingdom standard.

The enemy of our soul is a master at extremes. I really believe that he loves playing with the minds of people and having them go from one extreme to the next. When you recognize that you are a procrastinator but never assess how you are spending your time, you may miss the "shift" of moving over into the realm of laziness. When you assess how much time you spend wasting a day away because you're taking *naps* and not just one nap but *multiple naps or one long lengthy nap*, does it ever dawn on you what you could have accomplished in that time span? The enemy doesn't want you to even think twice about it. He desires that you keep moving right along at the pace of "kingdoms do nothing" so he can cause you to miss the window(s) of opportunity that are waiting on you.

Lethargy

1: abnormal drowsiness

2: the quality or state of being lazy, sluggish, or indifferent

Prophet Brian Carn Clarion Call 10/7/16 Periscope: "It's time for the church to hurry to the altar and pray! Playtime is over – we need to pray! The Spirit of God says those who are operating under the spirit of procrastination are about to miss what God is about to do. Make it your business to be sober and vigilant. Work while its day for at night no man can work. Time for you to stop being lazy. The Lord says 'Get Up!' The word of the Lord says to move and stop being slow to start your day (this was a rebuke to him he says because he is truly a night owl). God says to move and move quickly. Start praying and stop being lazy and get busy with what God has for you to do. God says the delay is over and He's about to move quickly."

The assignment is *prayer*, according to the word of the Lord through the prophet of God! So if we are waiting to the last minute and not being proactive, we can forfeit our Kingdom Assignment. We can't be nearly as effective *after the fact*! That would be like going into a ballgame after the final buzzer goes off! Who does that! When the window of opportunity has passed, it has passed.

"You must seize opportunities of a lifetime
during the lifetime of the opportunity."
Bishop Dale Bronner

"Then Jesus came with them to a place called Gethsemane, and He told the disciples, 'Sit here while I go over there and pray.' Taking along Peter and the two sons of Zebedee, He began to be sorrowful and deeply distressed. Then He said to them, 'My soul is swallowed up in sorrow to the point of death. Remain here and stay awake with me. 'Going a little farther, He fell facedown and prayed, 'My Father! If it is possible, let this cup pass from me. Yet not as I will, but as You will. 'Then He Came to the disciples and found them sleeping. He asked Peter, 'So, couldn't you stay awake with Me one hour? Stay awake and pray, so that you won't enter into temptation. The spirit is willing, but the flesh is weak." Again, a second time, He went away and prayed, 'My Father, if this cannot pass

unless I drink it, Your will be done." And
He came again and found them sleeping,
because they could not keep their eyes open.
After leaving them, he went away again and
prayed a third time, saying the same thing
once more. Then He came to the disciples
and said to them, 'Are you still sleeping and
resting? Look, the time is near. The Son of
Man is being betrayed into the hands of
sinners. Get up; let's go! See, My betrayer
is near." Matthew 26:36–46 (KJV)

Lethargy is not a kingdom mindset! Being drowsy or in a state of laziness, sluggishness or remaining indifferent does not reflect the mind of a believer that has been transformed or renewed. As believers, we are encouraged to awake from a place of passivity. God rewards our discipline of diligently seeking after him. This is the clarion call to rise up! Wake up! Wise up!

The area of procrastination is an old trick, an old habit, an old demon. It's a part of the arsenal of tricks, strategies and tactics that the enemy of our souls uses to keep us from walking in the place of excellence in which we were designed to walk.

Please take note of this last nugget that I must impart. Have you ever noticed how your flesh wants to rise up in almost any area where someone comes along and they are putting forth practices that show forth excellence that seemingly show you up? It's not that you're not as talented

105

or gifted, but they just seem to manage their time better; so their presentation almost always is a cut above yours. It's as if you had an idea but because you waited until the last minute you forgot to incorporate the idea, therefore you feel a little slighted because it would appear that you were outdone.

Well, my brother and my sister, put behind you those years of last minute shenanigans! Move forward with excellence, diligence and surround yourself with kingdom-minded movers and shakers. Be like the five wise virgins and be prepared for the bridegroom.

> *"Iron sharpeneth iron; so a man sharpeneth the countenance of his friend." Proverbs 27:17 (KJV)*

> *"As iron sharpens iron, so one man sharpens {and influences} another {through discussion}." Proverbs 27:17 (AMP)*

Be around those that will sharpen you, and relieve yourself of the need to go for the *3 C's*. Get delivered and set free from the spirit and mindset of procrastination! *"Don't compare! Don't compete! Don't complain!"*

Once you get free from the spirit and mindset of procrastination, you will find that there is no need to

Compete, Complain or Compare because whom the Son sets free is free indeed!

> *"If the Son therefore shall make you free, ye shall be free indeed." John 8:36 (KJV)*

Note(s) to self from this chapter

_____
_____
_____
_____
_____
_____
_____
_____
_____
_____
_____
_____
_____

Write your own personal daily affirmations

_____
_____
_____
_____
_____
_____
_____
_____
_____
_____
_____
_____
_____

There *Is* Help for the Procrastinator

Objective

To provide a clear, concise description of a procrastination and the mindset of one who procrastinates

An area where I had a lot of difficulty was asking for help. Oftentimes when there is something we need to complete or even when there is something that we have been mandated to do, we are reluctant to seek the assistance of others to get the job started and / or completed. In all honesty that is nothing more than the spirit of pride. We have to humble ourselves and ask for help – pray for God's help. In 2 Chronicles 7:14 the Lord says, "If my people, which are called by my name, shall humble themselves, and pray, and seek my face, and turn from their wicked ways; then will I hear from heaven, and will forgive their sin, and will heal their land." The Lord requires humility from us in order to get his help.

1. As with any habit, in order to overcome it you must admit that you have the habit. Own your issue! Recognize that you are engaging in an unhealthy practice.

> *"Agree with thine adversary quickly, whiles thou art in the way with him; lest at anytime the adversary deliver thee to the judge, and the judge deliver thee to the officer, and thou be cast into prison. Verily I say unto thee, Thou shalt by no means come out thence, till thou hast paid the uttermost farthing." Matthew 5:25, 26 (KJV)*

Within the justice system, there is such a thing as an out-of-court settlement. When one settles out of court, ordinarily, the matter whereby one is trying to settle is usually reached where a person can pay a smaller amount than what they actually owe. But in order to do so, one must respond quickly and not linger, because the longer you put it off, the worse the situation gets and the consequences may be more grave or severe.

How does this apply to procrastination? Well, the sooner you agree with the accuser of your soul that you have an issue in the area of procrastination, the sooner you will begin taking the necessary steps and actions to incite change. It becomes more difficult to change a habit the longer you allow the habit to linger, and the ability to change or come out of that particular habit – seemingly diminishes. Sure God can deliver you immediately! You, however, must still admit that you have an issue that you need His help in resolving.

2. Set Yourself Up For SUCCESS!

Here is a place where your action steps are going to be small goals that you set for yourself in order to see something new and different. There are several action steps you can take:

Having an accountability partner! Start by - Beginning projects on time or do a little on a project each day. Inform your accountability partner of your plans and require that they check in on you and follow up on your progress.

Have your accountability partner *"repeat out loud any excuse you may give them"* so that you can hear how *you sound making excuses.*

Say daily affirmations pertaining to completing your tasks or assignments!

3. Break big task up into small tasks. Putting off things until you just can't put it off any longer, winds up turning into this huge, insurmountable monument of a task – hence the Pileup. It would be nice to think that one day it won't be that way; but every time you put it off, it always winds up being just like the last thing you put off. So, the action step that I strongly suggest is… doing a little bit at the time.

Seriously! You already know that's the ticket to kicking this habit. Purpose in your heart and mind that you will do a little bit each day. Remember the key is a little at a time – put yourself on a time limit. You may want to start with ten minutes in the morning and ten minutes around noon, then finally ten minutes in the evening. Whatever you do, meet the challenge of breaking up the project into manageable tasks that you can accomplish in a short period of time.

The trick to this is, when we do it this way – we sense and see progress. Progress is a strong motivator for the procrastinator.

4. Reward yourself for accomplishing the small task. Pat yourself on the back and say "great job!" Praise yourself for taking steps towards change! You know your budget, you know what you like and dislike, and you know what it takes to make you smile. So, take advantage of your little accomplishment treats. It can be weekly, or how ever often you see fit to do something to keep you motivated and encouraged in order to move toward *change*.

Here's one of my treats to myself – I love to decorate. My favorite style of decorum is "Cottage Style." So, for a treat, I will get myself a "Cottage Style" magazine to oooh and ahhh over. I don't have to get one every time I reach a goal, but when I reach a small goal, I can sit down with my magazine and a glass of tea or diffused water. I can enjoy a few minutes doing what brings me a smile and a sense of peace. It's not a budget buster and it's something that pleases and rewards me for my small victory.

5. Don't be afraid to take advantage of help when you need it and when it is offered. Some of us don't have jobs where other people can really do anything to assist us. But, if you are fortunate enough to be in an environment or have close family and friends who can assist you with tackling a project; then by all means kick pride to the curb and yell for help!

6. Don't allow yourself to get so bogged down that you feel as though you are drowning! Be proactive! Take the initiative!

GLOSSARY

Block - to obstruct (someone or something) by placing obstacles in the way

Delay - verb (used with object) a situation in which something happens later than it should

: the amount of time that you must wait for something that is late

1. to put off to a later time; defer; postpone:

2. to impede the process or progress of; retard; hinder: verb (used without object)

3. to put off action; linger; loiter: *He delayed until it was too late.*

noun

4. the act of delaying; procrastination; loitering.

5. an instance of being delayed: *There were many delays during the train trip.*

6. the period or amount of time during which something is delayed:

Detain - verb (used with object)

1. to keep from proceeding; keep waiting; delay.

2. to keep under restraint or in custody.

3. *Obsolete.* to keep back or withhold, as from a person.

4. to restrain especially from proceeding

Diligence – the constant and earnest effort to accomplish what is undertaken; persistent exertion of body or mind.

Diligent – 1. Constant in effort to accomplish something; attentive and persistent in doing anything.

2. Done or pursued with persevering attention; painstaking:

Excellent – 1. Possessing outstanding quality or superior merit, remarkably good.

2. Archaic. Extraordinary, superior.

Extend - to increase the length or duration of; lengthen; prolong:

Grace: *a*: unmerited divine assistance given humans for their regeneration or sanctification

b: a virtue coming from God

c: a state of sanctification enjoyed through divine grace

2 a: approval, favor <*stayed in his good graces*>

b archaic: mercy, pardon

c: a special favor: privilege <*each in his place, by right, not grace, shall rule his heritage — Rudyard Kipling*>

d: disposition to or an act or instance of kindness, courtesy, or clemency

e: a temporary exemption : reprieve

Idle - : not working, active, or being used

: not having any real purpose or value

: not having much activity

Impede - : to slow the movement, progress, or action of (someone or something)

to retard in movement or progress by means of obstacles or hindrances; obstruct; hinder.

: to interfere with or slow the progress of

Lethargy

1: abnormal drowsiness

2: the quality or state of being lazy, sluggish, or indifferent

Postpone - to decide that something which had been planned for a particular time will be done at a later time instead

Selfishness - : having or showing concern only for yourself and not for the needs or feelings of other people

1 : concerned excessively or exclusively with oneself : seeking or concentrating on one's own advantage, pleasure, or well-being without regard for others

2 : arising from concern with one's own welfare or advantage in disregard of others *<a selfish act>*

Shelve – : to put (something) on a shelf

: to stop doing or thinking about (something) for a period of time

: to make (someone) unable to play or perform

SLOTHFUL - lazy, indolent, slothful mean not easily aroused to activity. lazy suggests a disinclination to work or to take trouble *<take-out foods for lazy cooks>*. Indolent suggests a love of ease and a dislike of movement or activity *<the heat made us indolent>*. Slothful implies a temperamental inability to act promptly or speedily when action or speed is called for *<fired for being slothful about filling orders>*.

Slow - *1a*: mentally dull: stupid *<a slow student>b*: naturally inert or sluggish

2a: lacking in readiness, promptness, or willingness *b*: not hasty or precipitate *<was slow to anger>*

3a: moving, flowing, or proceeding without speed or at less than usual speed *<traffic was slow>b*: exhibiting or marked by low speed *<he moved with slow deliberation>c*: not acute *<a slow disease>d*: low, gentle *<slow fire>*

4: requiring a long time: gradual *<a slow recovery>*

5: having qualities that hinder rapid progress or action *<a slow track>*

119

6a: registering behind or below what is correct <*the clock is slow*>b: less than the time indicated by another method of reckoning c: that is behind the time at a specified time or place

Stall – *1*: to debar temporarily especially from a privilege, office, or function <*suspend a student from school*>

2a: to cause to stop temporarily <*suspend bus service*>b: to set aside or make temporarily inoperative <*suspend the rules*>

3: to defer to a later time on specified conditions <*suspend sentence*>

4: to hold in an undetermined or undecided state awaiting further information <*suspend judgment*> <*suspend disbelief*

Stronghold - : an area where most people have the same beliefs, values, etc.: an area dominated by a particular group

Suspend - verb (used with object)

1: to hang by attachment to something above: *to suspend a chandelier from the ceiling.*

2: to attach so as to allow free movement: *to suspend a door on a hinge.*

3: to keep from falling, sinking, forming a deposit, etc., as if by hanging: *to suspend solid particles in a liquid.*

4: to hold or keep undetermined; refrain from forming or concluding definitely: *to suspend one's judgment.*

5: to defer or postpone: *to suspend sentence on a convicted person.*

6: to cause to cease or bring to a stop or stay, usually for a time: *to suspend payment.*

7: to cause to cease for a time from operation or effect, as a law, rule, privilege, service, or the like: *to suspend ferry service.*

8: to come to a stop, usually temporarily; cease from operation for a time.

9: to stop payment; be unable to meet financial obligations.

10: to hang or be suspended, as from another object: *The chandelier suspends from the ceiling.*

11: to be suspended, as in a liquid, gas, etc.

Table - to put on hold or postpone

Wave - to dismiss or put out of mind: <u>disregard</u> —usually used with *aside* or *off*

Other phrases all meaning the same as the aforementioned:

Give a rain check

Hold up

Lay over

Put on hold

Put on ice

Put on the back burner

Set aside

Prayer For Deliverance From Procrastination

Father, I come to you today in the name of Jesus. I exalt your name and acknowledge that your name is above every name and at the name of Jesus, every knee will bow and every tongue confess that you are Lord. Today, I come before you agreeing quickly with the adversary of my soul and I acknowledge that I have operated in the spirit of procrastination. I have put things and matters of importance off until the last minute. I confess that I have embraced a mindset that is not reflective of the Kingdom of God. I confess to you that I am aware, alert and appalled at the time I have wasted doing things of lesser importance to fulfill my personal agenda and desires. Today, I choose to REPENT. By your power and because of Your grace, I choose to walk in a new direction. Your word promises that You order the steps of the good. Your word instructs me to acknowledge You in all of my ways and you will direct my path. I realize, by Your grace, that the kingdom of God is at hand. I realize that the enemy of my soul has beguiled me and caused me to think that "time" is not of the essence and that it can be wasted. I am sorry for every second that I have not put my time to good use as an ambassador for Your kingdom or a representative of Your kingdom in the market place. I'm asking that You please restore unto me everything that the palmer worm, canker worm, caterpillar and locust have eaten and stolen. I forgive those who have enabled my behavior. I repent of using any excuses that would keep me from owning up to the part I have played in being negligent regarding the responsibilities with which You have entrusted me. Please forgive me for sleeping when I should have been working. Please forgive me for not being prepared for opportunities that you were granting and needing me to be in place for. As I confess my faults, I believe your word that you are faithful and just to cleanse me from all unrighteousness. And as you have forgiven me for the asking, I forgive myself and embrace your plan for my life. I thank you for sending Your Spirit to help me overcome all areas of weakness. I expect to walk in your power, with the aid of the Holy Ghost in areas of preparation and discipline concerning market place and kingdom assignments. I declare and decree that I will represent You in the spirit of excellence. I thank You that You will vindicate me and restore my mind, thoughts and habits to the mirror image of YOU. I believe by faith that as I align my thoughts, plans and actions with your word that You will get the glory out of my life and cause me to extend grace and help to those in need that have struggled with the spirit of procrastination. I break the back of the spirit of procrastination and forget those things that are behind as I press toward the mark of the prize of the high calling in Jesus Christ. Now Lord as I end this simple prayer to You, I ask that You continually remind me that You are a rewarder of those that diligently seek after You. And lest I forget, make me aware that "Being a follower of Jesus doesn't cover up bad work." I honor You and bless you.

In Jesus' Name

AMEN

About the Author

Becky's neice

Prophetess Ginger Johnson – Taylor is a native of Waycross, GA. She matriculated through St. Joseph's Academy, Waycross High School, GA Military College, Middle GA Technical College, Troy State University, GA Baptist Bible College and Wilberforce University. Ginger was an enlisted member of the United States Air Force where she served in the Armed Forces for one term. While in the service she met and married her husband, Isaac Taylor Jr. They have been married for over thirty years. Together they have two adult children and four grandchildren. Prophetess Taylor was called to ministry in July 1990. She is a licensed and ordained elder and was installed in the office of Prophet in 2013. Prophetess Taylor is a member of Greater New Hope Church of Christ Written In Heaven. She is a phenomenal teacher, preacher and workshop presenter. Prophetess Taylor is the founder and CEO of PGTM and R.A.W. – Real Answers 4 Women / Relevant Assessment of Wounds. Ginger has ministered all around the United States and as of recent she has traveled abroad to the Bahamas and will be going to South Africa to minister in the spring. Prophetess Taylor hosts a daily radio broadcast, Monday – Saturday, known as "The Decadent Café" on The New Joy 100.3 FM and hosts an Annual Women's Conference "iWorship" - which convenes annually on Labor Day Weekend. You can follow her on FB, Twitter, IG or visit her website iworshipgtm.com. Prophetess Ginger Taylor is a member Delta Sigma Theta Sorority, Inc.